P9-DDE-342

Linkletter Down Under

Books by Art Linkletter

People Are Funny
Kids Say The Darndest Things
The Secret World of Kids
Confessions of a Happy Man
Kids Still Say The Darndest Things
Kids Sure Rite Funny
A Child's Garden of Misinformation
Oops!
I Wish I'd Said That
Linkletter Down Under

LINKLETTER DOWN UNDER

by Art Linkletter

Illustrated by Paul Rigby

URE SMITH • SYDNEY • LONDON

First Published in the British Commonwealth in
1968 by Ure Smith Pty Ltd
155 Miller Street, North Sydney, NSW 2060
London office: Horwitz Group Books
88 Farringdon Street, EC4
First published in the United States of America
in 1968 by Prentice-Hall, Inc,
Englewood Cliffs, NJ 07632

National Library of Australia Registry
No. Aus 68-2782
Library of Congress Catalog Card No. 68-54550
This edition printed in Hong Kong

To indomitable Australia—
where the dynamics of change
and choice cause individualism
to be the force for doing
and freedom an urgent
state of mind

Foreword

In a sense this book is a small tribute to my lost friend Harold Holt.

The sea took his life when he launched his last adventure into the rolling Australian surf on December 17, 1967. He entered the water in the same spirit of restless boldness that marked his career as a world leader, as Prime Minister of his beloved Australia, and as an enduring symbol of Australian–United States friendship.

It is significant that the sea should have claimed him. In life he stood as a living champion of that last great land frontier of earth, Australia. In death he vanished into another of man's frontiers, the ocean, which completely surrounds Australia.

Harold Holt was to have written the foreword for this book. Instead, it is my sad duty to pay homage to the man who was responsible for my ventures in his "land down under." He was, in fact, the inspiration for this book.

I shall remember him best in the gracious warmth of "The Lodge," his official home in the capital city of Canberra. In particular, I recall one of our last visits there in October 1966. With Clyde Vandeburg and my son Jack, Lois and I were luncheon guests and had come to tell him about plans for this book and to report our progress in the development of cattle stations in the Australian Northwest. It was typical of the man and of his charming wife, Zara, that they were more interested in the informative potential of this book than in what we had accomplished as a result of our financial investment in Australia. The Holts were determined that the world should be made aware of Australia.

Clyde Vandeburg, who encouraged me to do this book and who worked with me in its production, makes a special contribution to this tribute that reflects the love and respect that Harold Holt earned from his fellow Australians. Evidence of this regard is contained in a letter Van received from our mutual friend, W. A. (Bill) Beattie of Melbourne.

An economist, agronomist, lecturer, and author, Bill has been both participant and observer in the growth and change of Australia under Harold Holt. He wrote to us on December 21, 1967:

"We have just witnessed one of the most moving events in the history of Australia . . . the Memorial Service in Saint Paul's Cathedral Church [Melbourne] for Harold Holt.

"It is not likely that such an event will occur again . . . and because it has meant so much it will not likely be forgotten . . . it was a tribute to a man who was an honorable politician, who wanted to see politics cleansed everywhere . . . who loved his fellowmen of whatever race or color . . . a true servant of the people and of the cause of the people. . . .

"He loved the sea and the sea took him. . . . Perhaps the gods of the sea knew that his death would create a profound impression that might draw, in closer bonds, those nations bordering the world's greatest ocean, the Pacific.

". . . I think this may have been the greatest gathering of Princes and Presidents and Heads of State that . . . [Australasia] has seen. . . . Some of them recently at war but here united to honor the name and purpose of a fine good man. . . . These great men came willingly and without hesitation. . . . To us they gain in stature for this spontaneous demonstration of respect.

"Another aspect affected us deeply . . . although the service took place in Saint Paul's Anglican Cathedral, present, and for the first time, were all faiths . . . Roman Catholics, the Bishops of the Greek and of the Russian Orthodox Churches, the Rabbis, . . . and the Heads of all Protestant denominations . . . all in their robes of office. It was more than a colorful sight. It was an earnest expression of the desire for the unity of all churches. This has never happened before in our country.

"We feel, therefore, that the death of Harold Holt has given great impetus to the urgency of bringing men together . . . a singleness of purpose that may unite the affairs of humanity. . . . We feel that Australia has come through its period of adolescence and that Harold Holt brought us to our majority.

"He has left us a legacy of purpose. . . ."

As a private citizen and as a government official, the late Prime Minister's faith in Australia's future greatness was constant. Harold Holt was a believer. Good on him!

CONTENTS

Linkletter Down Under

CHAPTER ONE

Australia Anyone?

The first time I ever gave a single serious thought to Australia was at a stag dinner party given by one of my close friends, Allen Chase, in his Bel Air home in southern California. The year was 1954. Among the guests was Australia's then Federal Treasurer, Harold Holt, an old friend of Allen's and mine, who had been invited to tell us about the "land down under."

Holt, an immensely warm and gregarious man, was brimming over with confidence in the future of his country. He spoke of it as a man speaks about the woman—or the horse—he loves: with enthusiasm, with pride, and with tender affection. It was, he said, the very last of the great frontiers.

"As the western United States was perhaps a hundred years ago," he told the guests, "so Australia is today—on the verge of a rich expansion. Nowhere else in the world is there a place where money invested today will pay such high dividends."

Between tales of kangaroos and high adventure in the outback, he told of his country's abundant natural resources and the millions of acres of untouched virgin land.

He told of one incident where a man, flying his private plane in Western Australia, was forced down in a remote canyon. He became curious about the red rock that made up the major land mass in the area and later he went back on foot to make a more thorough examination. The rock turned out to be iron ore, and tests indicated that there are perhaps fifteen billion tons of high-grade deposits in that area alone.

Holt vividly described real estate in Sydney, manufacturing in Melbourne, the excitement of Canberra, the new capital city, and the plans being made for damming the Ord River to create a vast new cotton-growing area in the northwest.

I knew very little about Australia before I went to that dinner party. When I thought about it at all, I visualized a great land mass of desert surrounded by a green coastal fringe. I did remember that when it was summer here, it was winter there. I knew rather vaguely that kangaroos, koala bears, eucalyptus trees, and some stone-age aborigines were indigenous to the country and that it was considered a continent, rather than an island. I realized that geographically and politically it was important to the United States and the free world. I knew that Australian soldiers were among the world's best fighters and that they wore wide-brimmed hats turned up on one side.

These things I vaguely knew, but I did not know any of the exciting things that Holt was telling us, or that Australia is about equal in size to the continental United States excluding Alaska, or that it has a population of little more than eleven million—about four persons to the square mile.

"That's what makes the place such a land of opportunity," Holt went on. "Australia is enormously rich and the riches are owned by so few people. We have the land, we have the natural resources, and we have the stable government. What we need now are men with know-how to get the riches out—and money. We need money to shrink the vast distances and we need money to build dams to hold water to irrigate the land. We need money to wrest ore from the rich earth and we need money to extract the minerals from the ore. We need money for roads and airports and factories and fertilizer. And we need money to provide men to do these things. The wealth of Australia is beyond belief, but it is in a gigantic vault which only money and manpower can break out."

Holt went on to say that Australia is perhaps the oldest land space on the face of the earth. Formed eons before man made his presence felt anywhere in the world, the area matured without him long after other areas of the world were heavily populated. Australia history is easily 500 million years old. Man is the last of the living newcomers, and he (the Australian aborigine) did not set foot on the continent down under until about 25,000 years ago.

"The first white man did not come," he said, "until the eighteenth century, which is just like day before yesterday. So, you see, we are a new country and prospects for our development are almost unlimited. Take the rich delta land in the Northern Territory near Darwin, for instance. Here there are tens of thousands of acres of land that, properly developed, could be made into a magnificent agricultural empire. Enough rice could be grown to supply most of the world's granaries year in and year out. The soil is as rich as the fabled Nile Valley, but ten times greater in size."

Those are a few of the things the Honorable Harold Holt told us that evening. I couldn't have known it then, but his glowing story was to have a profound impact on my life.

When a man is lucky enough, as I have been, to make money in excess of the needs of himself and his family, he is likely to look around for constructive and meaningful ways to put the surplus to work. Most of the guests around the table that night were in this category. Just as Mr. Holt's magnetic Pied Piper pitch infused me with enthusiasm, so too were the others caught up with the idea of doing something worthwhile and exciting in Australia.

We saw not only an opportunity to help feed the exploding world population, but, I must confess, a chance to invest in a scheme which would conceivably pay enormous dividends. It was a combination hard to beat. Of course it was a gamble, but gambling is one of man's instincts. And I had always had a deep-seated yearning to own land—the more of it the better. So when Mr. Holt talked of millions of acres being available to anyone who had capital and courage, I was hooked. I had the capital and I was eager to prove that I had the courage.

I guess every man at one time or another thinks about leaving his heirs something really solid, and the idea of developing a stake in Australia for future Linkletters appealed to me. I reasoned that money is an artificial product that can so easily become worthless, but good, productive land in a stable country is about as sure as anyone can get.

By the time we got around to the brandy and cigars that night, a number of us had determined to investigate this potential rice-to-riches bowl in the northern wilderness of Australia. We peppered the Australian Treasurer with questions. He told us that millions and millions of monsoon seasons had deposited rich layers of black topsoil along the coastal plains in the area of the Alligator River. The seasonal rainfall from December to March each year averages some sixty-five inches, and this uncontrolled flood of water comes down from the hills bringing layers of fertile soil which it deposits on the plain. It was Mr. Holt's conviction that almost anything would grow in it.

In contrast to so many politicians and promoters, our Australian friend was fully prepared to back up his glowing statements with action by his government. Speaking as the right-hand man of Prime Minister Robert Menzies, he assured us that hundreds of thousands of acres could be ours if we would develop it.

You know how it is when you get hooked on an idea. I saw myself standing up to my belt in rice. In whatever direction I looked and as far as I could see there was waving grain, green in contrast to the black soil and the blue sky. Plows were ploughing, reapers were reaping, trucks were being loaded with rice, and freight ships were carrying the grain to all of the world's hungry people.

It was an exciting and beautiful picture to a city man with a yen to live close to the soil, and when Allen Chase suggested that a syndicate be formed to make an examination of the rich Northern Territory delta, I was one of the first to volunteer. Among the other original investors were Charles Correll, famous for his portrayal of Andy in the radio classic "Amos 'n' Andy," and Robert Cummings, the movie star.

Three actors and a banker! And guess what we called ourselves! By the romantic and grandiloquent title the "Hollywood Pioneers"! More suitable, as things turned out, would have been "Babes from Hollywood."

Our first hurdle in this new venture was to overcome our appalling ignorance of agriculture in general. Bob Cummings had never even grown a geranium. Allen Chase's beautiful garden was tended by two full-time gardeners and three helpers. Charles Correll had been a bricklayer before rising to fame in radio. And the closest I had come to agriculture was working briefly on a wheat-combine team in the Middle West as a kid. The most any of us knew about rice was that it was great with chicken and almonds at Trader Vic's restaurant.

Admittedly, our knowledge was slim and our collective agricultural experience was less than slight, but we were loaded with optimism. Not only were we going to solve the world's hunger problem but there was a good chance that we would all go down in history as great humanitarians. We had it bad—but good.

That very same evening we put together a fund to get started on the Big Adventure Down Under. Motivated by what must have been the same romantic vision that prompted our pioneer forefathers to quit jobs in banks, sell their homes, cash in their insurance, buy Conestoga wagons, and head westward during the mid-1800's, we modern-day Hollywood Pioneers proceeded in the following months to negotiate a land contract with the Australian Government, hire agronomists, agriculturists, engineers, scientists, and accountants and send them to Darwin in our crusade for rice. As further evidence of our romanticism, we informally called our expedition *Project Marco Polo,* a gesture of defiance aimed primarily at my partner-friend Clyde Vandeburg who coined the title to indicate his skepticism.

It was late, after midnight, when I got home from the Chase dinner, and though I tried to be quiet, my wife, Lois, was awake when I came into our bedroom.

"Is that you, Art?" she asked, and I countered with, "Are you awake?" (Someday I must compile a book of questions that require no answers.)

"Did you have a good time?" she asked.

That was all the opening I needed and said, "Guess what! We're going to Australia!"

"Australia!" She sat straight up in bed.

"Yes, we're going to raise rice—enough to feed the Orient and maybe the whole world. Just think of it!"

Lois stared at me and then she said, "Art, what *have* you been drinking?"

"I couldn't be more sober nor more serious," I rushed on. Using my best sales technique, since my wife has tremendous sales resistance when it comes to some of my schemes, I began telling her what Harold Holt had related at the Chase dinner party.

Somewhere in my story Lois interrupted me. "But Art," she almost wept, "you're already up to your ears in cattle ranches and ski resorts and retirement homes and who knows what all—to say nothing of your television shows and books. You don't have an hour to spare as it is. How in Heaven's name are you going to squeeze in Australia?"

She had a point, and as usual, logic was on her side. It was a venture I knew absolutely nothing about; Australia is sixteen hours away by jet; my schedule was jammed for months ahead with personal appearances, board meetings, and TV shows. My wife thoroughly disapproved.

Naturally, I decided to go ahead.

CHAPTER TWO

Westward Who? Me?

As Head Scout of the Hollywood Pioneers, Allen Chase negotiated with the Australian Government for the hundred thousand acres we intended to develop. The price was right—nothing. There was just one little proviso: we had to pay for dams, roads, leveling, ploughing, seeding, and harvesting. We were to build homes, import workers, and buy vast amounts of machinery.

By the time the land contracts had been signed, our original group had been enlarged to include Samuel Mosher, President of Signal Oil Company; Ralph Davies, President of American President Lines; Robert Hixson, an advertising executive; Jack Tyler, President of Farmer's Insurance Group; Christopher Holmes, heir to a Fleischmann yeast fortune; and the late Dutch Kindelberger, President of North American Aviation. Several Australians also came in, headed by Paul Cullen, a former member of the Australian Air Force and presently a Sydney investor and businessman. Cullen was to be the syndicate's man-on-the-spot and would supervise the overall operation from Sydney, almost two thousand miles from Darwin.

Rice experts from nearby Queensland and distant Thailand were consulted as to what kind of rice would be best suited to the climate and most in demand in the markets of Asia. The long-grain rice of Thailand was chosen, and the frustrating struggle to get seed into the country past the vigilant Australian inspectors began.

Of all the places in the world where government controls concerned with admitting man, beast, fruit, plant, or seed are stringent, Australia is the toughest. The Aussies regard with jaundiced eye and clamped jaw the admission of anyone or anything that might bring to their isolated land a disease or parasite which could adversely affect their way of life.

I recently thought of this Australian fixation while standing in the customs office in Sydney eating a small packet of cooked, salted sunflower seeds which I was not permitted to bring into the country. And I remembered that the 1962 Olympic games were staged without equestrian events because Australian law insisted that horses be quarantined for six months before being admitted, because of the possibility of brain fever. Even badly needed bull semen may not be brought into the country for cattle breeding because scientists cannot guarantee that it does not carry the feared "blue tongue" disease which might destroy the sheep on whose backs so much of Australia's wealth rides. Recently a fellow American was aghast to see his favorite Western riding saddle completely dismantled stitch by stitch for fumigating before he could bring it in, and he never got it put together to suit him.

Because of the Aussies' exacting laws, almost half of our original consignment of seed was "treated" to the point of being rendered infertile. Out of the seed we salvaged that first year, we succeeded in planting only 5 acres of rice, a mere "Victory garden" patch in that vast wilderness of 100,000 acres. But the end result was good. The rice plants were sturdy and prolific, so we were lured on to a further effort. Ten acres of rice planted in 1956 rewarded us with a good-sized harvest of the precious seed. Now we were ready to go for broke. Literally.

So far, we Hollywood Pioneers had enjoyed our Marco Polo adventure along the Alligator River from a safe distance of twelve thousand miles. To be sure, Allen Chase had made the long journey every few months to check on the work and report the progress. Meanwhile the rest of us went about our daily affairs buoyed by the good reports. But the time had come for us to make a triumphant trip to Australia for the ceremony of kicking off the first really big crop. We were ready to plant a thousand acres! Our vision of feeding the world's hungry was about to get under way in earnest.

Flying to Australia from California over the vast reaches of the Pacific must be somewhat like going to the moon, except that every now and then for a brief hour you put down on an island for fuel. The time changes are especially hard on the brain's clockwork mechanism. You are getting up in Australia when you should be going to bed, and crossing the international date line in mid-Pacific going west you lose a day of your life. Coming back, you live the same day twice, which is rather intriguing. Even more confusing, the seasons of the two hemispheres are exactly opposite.

When night came, the sense of loneliness was intensified by an arrangement of stars that I had never before seen. No Castor and Pollux, no Big Dipper, no Seven Sutherland Sisters. But I did recognize the constellation called the Southern Cross.

After a stopover in Hawaii, we settled on the beam at 31,000 feet for the long voyage to Fiji. We felt infinitesimally small between the marshmallow cloud below, which lay like a child's dream of heaven, and the blue, blue sky above. Indeed we seemed so detached from reality, we might as well have been on our way to Pluto. Occasionally when the clouds parted, the smooth emptiness of the ocean between Hawaii and Fiji was broken by feathery waves breaking over an emerging coral reef.

Fiji is a "free port" where you can buy such things as French perfumes, Japanese cameras, shell beads, German tape recorders, and Swiss watches at bargain prices because you don't have to pay import duties on them.

The local British wear starched white shirts and shorts with white knee socks. The Fijians wear a wraparound skirt and have bushy, kinky hairdos. The native Fiji people are friendly and helpful and they have a great sense of humor. They love to laugh about how Great-grandpa gobbled the missionary, though if you really pin them down they will admit that there weren't nearly as many people popped in the boiling pot as Westerners are led to believe. The natives have a social system that is pure and simple communism. What's yours is mine and what's mine is yours. If I ask you for something, you have to give it to me and I don't have to give it back. Sounds like a great idea for handling the mother-in-law problem.

Fiji is on the international date line and the moment we took off we hopped from Friday to Sunday. It so happens that Saturday is my favorite day of the week, and as we flew along I thought of all the things I might have done with the lost day. Of course, thinking about it abstractly, the whole day would surely have been very constructive and the loss seemed a pity. I don't remember what exactly I did with the day gained on the return trip.

Meals get very mixed up on the long flight to Australia. We had already had four meals in a twelve-hour period and when it seemed like we should have been having dinner, breakfast was served. We had fresh pineapple, broiled ham, poached egg, fresh stewed tomatoes, warm hard rolls, cheese, and tea. They sure didn't want us to starve! The napkin was equipped with a plastic hook so it could be hung from the collar. I had been taught that tucking the napkin in one's collar was not a mannerly thing to do, but I learned that it is an accepted aerial custom in Australia. It seems to be indicative of the Australian's ability to keep his equilibrium in turbulent air while flouting the social graces. There is nothing effete about these people. They take delight in reducing social niceties to the practical lowest common denominator. I don't mean that they are rude in any way; far from it. Australians in their brusque way are one of the most polite people on earth. Certainly they are among the most genuine, and they don't do much of anything just for "looks" or surface effect.

Four hours and a half by jet from Fiji brought us to Sydney. Of all Australian cities, Sydney is the largest, having a population of 2.3 million. A swaggering, boisterous beehive with a beautiful natural setting, it has one of the world's great deep-water harbors. More than any other place I know, including the spectacular bridge which serves as its landmark, it reminds me of San Francisco. Its beaches are wide stretches of warm sand; its shops are full of the world's merchandise; its mutton, native oysters, crayfish, and huge prawns are superb; and I do not believe Australian beer is surpassed anywhere. (Cautionary note: Two glasses per new arrival is the limit since the alcoholic content is a sturdy 7 percent.)

Sydney is a bustling, bubbling, busy city, where the weather is delightful—an average of 342 sunny days a year. Rising above the harbor in the city's center is a beautiful park which is hemmed by rather ordinary looking buildings. Nearby, however, are charming structures created by Australia's first major architect, Francis Howard Greenway, who had come to the land down under as a convict. He was pardoned by the governor because the new country needed his talent, and to show his appreciation he designed the exquisite St. James Church, which was built in 1819. It is a precious link between Sydney's disreputable past and its thriving present.

No description of Sydney would be proper without mentioning its spectacular opera house, one of the most remarkable buildings in the world. It was designed by the Danish architect Joern Utzon, whose concept was chosen from hundreds of architectural designs submitted from all over the world. It rises on a site which juts into the harbor and will contain within its shells of precast concrete two halls and several theaters of varying sizes—that is, if it is ever finished. It has been abuilding now for years and is still far from completion. So far, $90 million has been budgeted to do the job, but no one really gets too upset because the money comes from a government-run lottery and who ever saw an Australian unwilling to "tyke a chance." One minor problem for the controversial opera house, a space for parking cars, was solved in a plan for four levels of underground parking, to be housed beneath part of the site. The shape of the building is most revolutionary, and nobody has the slightest idea whether its acoustics will be more suitable to Swiss yodeling than to opera.

One thing is certain: It provides good conversation with the local cab drivers. Australian taxicabs are exceptional, I think, because they charge the lowest fares in the world: twenty cents when the flag goes down and eighteen cents a mile. On the other hand, like New York cab drivers, the Sydney "hacker" will give you an opinion on anything from a scandal in King's Cross to the war in Vietnam. He may not know everything, but he'll make it sound as if he does.

King's Cross is Sydney's Greenwich Village. The time to see it, of course, is at night. The tiny bars, intimate night clubs, striptease joints, and rouged *dames du pavé,* make for what might be called a sinful section. Bearded poets, guitar-carrying beatniks, heterogeneous restaurants, and the musical mixture of foreign tongues and accents give the section a sort of carnival flavor.

Australians are generally not chic dressers. As a rule, the women are neatly dressed but certainly their costumes are not featured in *Vogue* magazine. Many of the men wear comfortable jeans and windbreakers or long coat-sweaters rather than jackets. When they do wear jackets they are given to decorating them with buttons or fraternity badges in the lapels. When I arrived at the Menzies Hotel in Sydney, I encountered a shuffleboard team from Coral Gables, Florida. The players wore bright orange jackets emblazoned with a pocket patch that depicted crossed coconut palms framing a shuffleboard court with a gold sun presumably sinking in the west. These casually dressed fellow countrymen did not seem out of place at all, for a great number of the men and women I saw during my sojourn in the city (with the exception of businessmen) appear to have formed a marked preference for wearing casual clothes, whatever their occupation might be.

In the bar at the Menzies Hotel, cocktails of two jiggers of I. W. Harper cost sixty cents. Australian whiskey, it is generally conceded, is dreadful; even the Australians refuse to drink it. The bartender at the Menzies told me he sold fifty bottles of American bourbon to one of Aussie whiskey.

Along with the drinkers, though, there are the wowsers—the church supporters, the blue-law-passers, and the do-gooders—who are equally bold and tireless. There is a wide streak of puritanism in the Australian character.

Labor unions are strong in Australia and union members are notorious for their lack of inhibition. Recently the Sydney longshoremen demanded "temptation money"—a kind of bonus—for unloading Scotch whisky.

I was struck by the tanned Australian men. They are lean and relaxed with the rough humor one associates with Rocky Mountain Westerners. Both sexes look athletic and healthy and there is an easy camaraderie between them, so much so, in fact, that the girls seem almost boyish. Because of this, something of the mystery of romance is lost. Love doesn't seem to be the emotional obsession in Australia that it is in our country. Women are not regarded as second-class citizens as they are in much of the Orient, but they are not venerated either. The Aussie woman seems to have less control over and gets less attention from her man than the American woman. Perhaps this explains to some extent the Australian woman's air of genuine independence.

Anyone visiting Australia for the first time will find himself passing through three stages in his relations with the people there. First, you will be effusively welcomed with open arms and a "what took you so long to get here" attitude. The handclasps will be strong, the hospitality gracious, and you will almost literally be swept off your feet. But then comes the second stage. Without meaning to, you will say something or do something that touches an Aussie nerve and he will bristle. When this happens you will find yourself not the warmly held comrade but the excluded stranger. Stage three comes when you are taken for granted. Then you have been accepted. And if an Australian begins finding fault with you, you're "in."

Because the Australian is a great equalizer, he neither praises nor creates heroes. No matter what your talent, unless you are a great athlete, you will awe no one. I know. One of the first comments about my television status came from a casual acquaintance. In a friendly tone he said, "Nobody here knows you from a ton of coal." Although I appear frequently on Australian television, I might as well have been a shoe clerk to the hotel barber, who incidentally charged me eighty cents for a haircut, up from fifty cents before World War II. Though my shoes were scuffed, I couldn't have them shined because there are no shoeshine boys in Sydney, except in hotels. And manicurists, I discovered, are few and far between.

I was fascinated one night when Clyde Vandeburg and I watched seven venturesome Australian lads in a tiny little Italian restaurant. They had a quart of beer and a quart of wine apiece. One fellow wasn't able to master the art of rolling spaghetti on his fork, and one of his companions said, "Mate, you aren't grounded right. Pass over your worms and I'll show you." He then proceeded to wind the spaghetti onto the fork against a large spoon. "You have to corner it with your fork," he instructed, "and lay it away with your spoon."

When first heard, the Australian accent sounds harsh to most Americans. It carries overtones of cockney but has a lilt all its own. It is raffish and sardonic with a lighthearted disrespect for authority. Somehow it is perfectly suited to the Aussie temperament.

It is not the accent, though, that distinguishes the Aussie speech; it is the lack of enunciation. Running words together is called "Strine," which translates into "Australian." "Let stalk Strine" means "Let's talk Australian."

You soon catch onto the game of speaking Strine, so when you hear someone say, "Aorta build another arber bridge," you know it means "We ought to build another harbor bridge." "Baked necks" is the Strine way of ordering bacon and eggs. And Australians seem to live on a diet of "stike an' aigs."

"Garment seamy anile seaward icon do" is an invitation, and if you read it aloud its meaning will become clear.

"I gunga din—the door slokt!" means you're locked out, and "sly drool" is an instrument used by engineers.

A British author, appearing in a Sydney shop to autograph her book, was handed a copy by a woman who said, "Emma chisit." Thinking this was the purchaser's name, the author wrote, *To Emma Chisit,* on the flyleaf and signed her name. It turned out the customer had merely asked for the price of the book in Strine.

Of course, there are words that have their own special meaning, far different from the original English intent. "Crook" means bad, or poor, as on a rainy morning, you will hear the phrase "It's a crook day." Sydney citizens, who take a dim view of their conservative neighbors down in Melbourne, call them wowsers. While we might use this term to describe a hell-raiser or a rake, the Sydney citizen uses it to scorn the Melbournite as a "blue nose," a prig, or an ultra-conservative.

Even more than Americans, Australians have always had a passion for equality. The Aussie does not take kindly to snobbishness or hypocrisy and he cannot stand a stuffed shirt. This attitude possibly dates back to the convict period. Australia was claimed for the British by Captain James Cook in 1770. In 1779 Sir Joseph Banks, who had accompanied Cook, suggested to the British Government that Australia would be a fine dumping place for English convicts. Subsequently several hundred malfeasants were put ashore at what is now Sydney. A quarter of the convicts were women, and a third of these were professional harlots. By 1868, when the transportation of convicts was abolished, some 168,000 such wrongdoers had been shipped to Australia, many of them hardened criminals. Thus many of Australia's founding fathers were transgressors and this may explain certain aspects of the Australian character—their camaraderie, particularly in the face of hardship, their tendency to be pugnacious, and their strong resentment of authority.

One might assume that Australians, like our own San Franciscans, would like to gloss over this part of their past, and some of them do. But others bend the truth a bit to their own advantage when they trace their ancestry. I've heard many a proud Aussie claim his pioneer forefathers were "the most select group of people in England; each one was carefully selected by a sentencing judge." Other proud "diggers" point out that many idealistic, adventurous Irishmen were among

Nor'west waterhole.

the volunteers who sailed halfway around the world to found a new nation.

And, of course, there were the famed "remittance men" whose wealthy, titled families paid them a handsome yearly sum to go to Australia and stay out of their hair for good. The story is told that one of these perennial black sheep wrote home to London that he'd finally married one of the native Australians and his mother was supposed to have thrown up her hands in horror and remarked, "Imagine having a kangaroo in our family!"

Although Australians rise dutifully to the first stanza of "God Save the Queen," they generally don't have much allegiance to that imperial lady. The umbilical cord between England and Australia was cut long ago, and the wound has pretty well healed. Australia is still part of the British Commonwealth and on public occasions the Union Jack is displayed along with the Australian flag, but the attitude of Australians toward the English is highly equivocal. Though Australians may be attached to their British cousins, this attitude is largely sentimental; and in fact Australians are inclined to be somewhat hostile to the English. They use a scornful nickname, "pommie," to describe them. This odd word "pommie" has several possible beginnings. One of my outback buddies argues that it comes from the red cheeks of the British—a red color like pomegranates. Another Aussie friend told me that the early English soldiers wore pompons on their hats, and thus the word pommie. The most logical explanation came from a lady historian who confided to me at a Canberra cocktail party that the initials P.O.M. were originally stamped on the shirt of arriving convicts, identifying them as a "Prisoner of His Majesty."

CHAPTER THREE

Outback Blues

From Sydney we flew to Darwin, 2,500 miles away. This is no small hop. It's about like going across the United States from Miami, Florida, to Seattle, Washington. Sydney is in the southeast on the shore of the Tasman Sea, while Darwin is in the northwest on the Timor Sea.

The impact of Australia from the air is almost beyond comprehension. A few minutes out of Sydney and we saw no more farm patterns; there were few fences, and almost no roads. Hour after hour there was nothing beneath us but majestic desolation. I was filled with awe and a certain growing apprehension at the immeasurable nothingness. For the first time I sensed the awesome loneliness of utter, empty space.

The Australian aborigine's mystic, unrecorded religion has a legend that in the beginning Australia was too big to permit space between earth and sky. The sky hung so close upon the land, the legend goes, that the first men who came here, probably over land bridges from the north, had to crawl on their bellies. One stone-age man, yearning to stand up, gathered sticks and began to prop up the sky as if it were a tent. And although the weight of the sky bent his sticks, he was at last able to stand up in a little space and walk about.

The bent boomerang is a part of that legend. It is considered a symbol of the stone-age aborigine's triumph over the brooding land.

Today, we fly by jet from Sydney to Darwin in approximately three hours and fifteen minutes. When we Hollywood Pioneers first made the hop to the Top End, it was by a combination of converted war-surplus DC-3's and 7's. The flying time was a torturous seven to ten hours depending upon the whim of pilot, weather, and equipment. Kangaroo time would have been safer and almost as fast.

The huge property we Hollywood Pioneers had acquired was part of a tiny speck on the map called Humpty Doo, a stretch of lush lowland carved into a thousand natural paddies and backwaters by the sinuous, many-channeled Alligator River. Humpty Doo is near Darwin in the tropical monsoon belt. Darwin's population of 12,500 is the most polyglot in Australia. Its inhabitants are rough, tough adventurers, crocodile hunters, government men, shippers, and aborigines who call themselves Top Enders. These people drink more beer per capita, play more dart games, and have more dog fights, I guess, than anyone else in the world. They live in tiny, scattered houses, most of which have corrugated tin roofs and open sides strongly screened against flies and mosquitoes. In lieu of air conditioning and in defense against termites, these abodes are usually perched on stilts. The red dirt streets glow in the heat of the tropical sun.

When we landed at the tiny International Airport, several passengers who were going on to Singapore and beyond followed me into the hotel bar. One of them sat down on the stool next to me and ordered Scotch and soda in a tall glass with lots of ice. "Man's only defense against the heat out here," he said. He lived in Hong Kong and was in the shipping business.

"But ships are too damned slow," he said, "so I travel in airplanes. This Darwin has got to be the tail end of creation," he added, looking around. "The Aussies ought to give it back to the aborigines. What the hell brings you out here?"

"I'm involved in a rice-growing scheme," I said.

"Rice! Here?"

I nodded, smiling at his surprise.

"You can't be serious."

"Cross my heart," I said. "We're going to grow enough rice in these parts to feed the world."

My companion tossed his drink down as the departure of his plane was called over the loudspeaker. "You bloody Yanks will do anything for kicks or a dollar," he said, and took one of his business cards from his pocket. "If you make a go of it, don't forget—I'm in the shipping business." And he hurried away, shaking his head.

Tropical, flavorful Darwin has one of the finest small harbors in the world. It has the strategic location to link the nation by trade with Asia, but it is locked from growth by the great brown land's forbidding interior geography. Originally, Darwin was settled as a port for the ocean shipment of cattle from the north end to other parts of Australia and the Far East. As such it became a government outpost where *somebody* had to stay, if only to collect taxes for His Majesty the King. Long since, the "killing plant," or slaughterhouse, has been abandoned and the cattle pens left in disrepair. Cattlemen preferred, because it was faster, to drive their herds the two thousand miles from the Top End to Brisbane.

I looked down on the harbor from the air and saw the whole surrounding area strewn with the wreckage of ships. I remembered that in 1942 the Japanese attacked and bombed Darwin as they had Pearl Harbor. It was here that the Japanese hoped to establish a beachhead for conquering all of Australia. Australian and United States Navy vessels prevented this in the Coral Sea Battle, whose anniversary is celebrated annually by the grateful Australians.

The easygoing, don't-harbor-any-grudges Aussies have since contracted with the Japanese to recover for scrap the metal of these ships which clog Darwin's harbor. "They gave it to us," a pub owner commented. "Might as well turn a bob and sell it back to them." The wartime hostility of the Australians toward the Japanese is pretty well gone, understandably, in view of the tremendous economic leverage the Japanese exert. Japan is now Australia's biggest customer. England is second, with the United States a strong and growing third.

Speaking of "turning a bob," following the success of the two small experimental rice plantings at Humpty Doo, we hired William Gunn to boss Project Marco Polo. Bill was a grazier and owned large pastoral properties in New South Wales. He was a director of a bank and had been recommended to us by Deputy Prime Minister John McEwen, head of the small but important Country party. While Gunn had never grown rice before, we thought his wide experience in business and agriculture would ensure the success of the venture at Humpty Doo. Bill picked me up in one of our new jeeps and drove me out to the property.

That ride to Humpty Doo was my first lesson in Australia's incredible natural history. We drove past actual termite cities consisting of towering structures designed and built by these most amazing insect architects. Some of the "apartment houses" built by the blind insects loom twenty feet above the ground. They have the hardness of concrete and a durability that stands for centuries against wind, sand, and monsoon torrents. These sculptured fantasies are remarkable, not only for their immensity and perfection but because they follow a plan of design that is consistent with the needs and habits of the occupants.

One of the many fascinating and as yet unanswered riddles concerning these termite construction workers is their apparent possession of a scientific knowledge of astronomy. The upright axes of the tall structures *always* lie approximately north and south, obviously to gain advantage and protection from the changing location of the sun. We know, for example, that in the morning the termites move to the eastern, or warm, side of their houses and to the shaded side in the afternoon. Furthermore, at noonday, when the sun is overhead, the knife-edge design of the termite structure exposes it to a minimum of heat.

There is no doubt that protection from heat is necessary,

even for termites, for this is hot country, this northern Australia, and as we bounced over the rough, dusty road, I commented on that fact.

"This is nothing," Bill Gunn said in much the manner of our own Texans. "It's only about a hundred degrees. Wait until it hits a hundred and twenty before you begin complaining." He went on to say that this was The Dry, a period of nine months during which no rain falls. During the other three months of the year—called The Wet—he said that sixty inches of rain would probably fall. The temperature remains about the same the year round—*hot!*

In the months immediately ahead I was to learn a great deal more about The Wet and The Dry. In fact, much, much more than I would care to know! And I learned quite a lot about Australia's flora and fauna too.

The property the Australian Government had made available to our American group comprised 100,000 acres along the coast of the Timor Sea and on both sides of the Alligator River. Why the river is called the Alligator is a mystery because there are no alligators along the coast of Australia, although there are innumerable crocodiles. The difference is that, though both are members of the lizard family, the croc has a long slender snout as compared to the alligator's broader jaw. The saltwater croc grows to twenty-six feet in length and can drag a full-grown cow under water to his lair. Inland crocs are harmless, much smaller, and, of course, of the freshwater variety.

Australia has varieties of crocodiles that are different from those found anywhere else in the world. The South American and African crocodiles are more cumbersome beasts in that their backbones are directly connected to their heads, and this prevents them from turning in a space less than their own length. The backbone of the Australian crocodile, on the other hand, stops at the shoulders, giving the Aussie croc his deadly suppleness, and enabling him to throw his fearsome jaws sideways or forward without having to move his body. I never went swimming no matter how hot it became!

Although the Australian croc's principal foods are fish and crabs, he will attack and devour any animal, including man, that comes within striking distance. His method of catching fish is ingenious. He will lie for hours in a pool or stream, his tail barely touching the bank. Thus his body creates a natural trap for fish feeding along the shore. Once the fish gets within range, the croc, with a scything sweep of the tail, will flip the victim onto the bank. With one pounce he then comes ashore and has the fish in his jaws. On the other hand, the croc often catches cows in exactly the opposite style. With beady eyes just above the surface of the water, he will study the watering times and habits of the livestock. Then, the wily croc will hide onshore behind a log or bush until the beast he's stalking bends its head to drink at the riverbank. With surprising speed the monster slithers down the shore, slaps the cow a mighty blow, driving it out into the water, and then dives in and drags it under water to marinate and age for a few days before devouring it.

The arrangement of the crocodile's teeth and the power of his jaw are deadly beyond compare. The teeth are conical in shape and each tooth in the lower jaw precisely meshes with teeth in the upper jaw. When the monster closes his mouth the combination of cutting and crushing power is incredible. One other interesting fact: A croc's eyes are shielded by external lids with a semitransparent third membrane, which protects the creature's eyes and still permits him to see underwater.

Crocodiles notwithstanding, the acreage we had been accorded was, to a fellow like me whose previous land holdings were measured in terms of subdivisions, a sizable chunk of soil. One hundred thousand acres took us to Australia, and then, if I may make a painful funny, those acres just took us.

Earth bores had been drilled in many places on the property, and they indicated that the rich alluvial soil had a depth of as much as eighty-five feet! Truly, neither the fabled fertile crescent nor the Nile River Valley had anything richer in the way of seedbed. The climate came with a guarantee of frost-free nights and intensely hot days, a combination that is just right for rice plants; and there was little possibility of hurricanes, tornadoes, or tidal waves. Earthquakes were the only other hazard we could think of, but no serious earthquakes have been recorded in Australia.

In other words, we couldn't lose. And a good thing, too, because we had spared no initial expense. We had hired rice experts, soil experts, irrigation experts, and *expert* experts. We vaguely realized there would be problems and disappointments, but with the natural hazards narrowed down through expertise to what we thought was the infallibility of dollars, you can imagine our optimism.

Bill told us, as we rode along, how the Australian Government had discovered rice would grow at Humpty Doo. In years gone by, he said, Chinese workers, brought to Darwin to build its port and railroad, had carelessly dropped grains of rice where they had paused to eat. Soon these rice grains took root voluntarily and continued to grow wild, completely unaided by cultivation.

"Think," said Bill, "what can be accomplished with scientific methods! You are participating," he went on, "in an enterprise that will have an importance far beyond these borders. This Top End is sure to become an agricultural empire!"

The Australian Government, I repeat, was vitally interested in what we were trying to do, and in fact, just about everyone in Australia wanted the "rice scheme," as the Aussies called it, to succeed. You couldn't have found anyone anywhere who would have been so foolish as to predict that it would fail.

Great cloud banks of smoke that hung over the land stirred my curiosity. Everywhere this strange pall of smoke arose from the outback. Some of the smoke, Bill explained, was coming from brush fires which had been purposely set by our men who were clearing the ground of grass and brush. Other fires had been set by outback stockmen to burn off the grasses and thereby rid the earth of billions of ticks which cling to the tips of dry vegetation while waiting to drop off onto a passing cow. Still other fires were set by aborigines to flush out wild game or to uncover the edible worms and slugs which burrow into

Rice!!! Early enthusiasts.

the earth to escape the heat of the sun. The mushrooming umbrellas of smoke are a perpetual phenomenon of the Top End during The Dry. And coming from smoggy Los Angeles, it made me just a little homesick!

Bill said that once the ground had been cleared at Humpty Doo, the earth dams bulldozed into place, and the rice planted, the area would become a paradise. It turned out that there was much he didn't know about paradise *or* the Top End.

For one thing, neither he nor any of us had figured on the ravaging abilities of the magpie goose. Did I put that in the singular? Well, make it plural. And add their friends, relatives, progeny, and in-laws. They are called magpie because of their mottled, black and white plumage which is similar to our American magpies. They should be called gobblers, because they are phenomenally expert at gulping down rice.

To our dismay, we learned that for centuries the geese had been coming to Humpty Doo to feed on the tender green wild plants which spring up each year following the monsoon rains. This year, sweeping in from the Arafura Sea and the Pacific Ocean, they discovered to their boundless joy that some kindly Hollywood Pioneers had anticipated their ravenous hungers and planted an extra-succulent dish—long-grain rice from Thailand. In fact, so eager were some of the early arrivals for this ambrosia they were happy to eat the seed as it was being planted, without waiting for any sprouting. And when experimental seeding was attempted from airplanes, there was added for the geese the fun of aerial acrobatics performed as they gobbled the beautiful grains before they even hit the ground. Sort of refueling in midair, you might say.

This was a most happy time for the bird population of northern Australia. To the multitude of wild fowl, which had blackened the skies by the end of February, Humpty Doo became known as the Hollywood Pioneer Australian Restaurant and Buffet Service. One of the brighter and obviously more indefatigable members of the Pioneers capitalized on this by suggesting that perhaps we had the wrong objective. Instead of

Rice!!! Hunter: *"Go on, just one more grain!"*

steamed rice for the tables of the world, we should be providing roast goose prestuffed with rice.

We must have killed a million of the birds. Hunters were invited and they came in droves. There was no limit. The geese were like the Mormon crickets in Utah. One hunter claimed he killed twenty-nine with one shot. "At least, that's how many I picked up," he vowed. "I don't know how many the dingoes got," referring to the wild dog which came to Australia long ago from Asia as the domesticated companion of the aborigine.

In a desperate effort to shoo the geese away, we tried noisemakers of various kinds, including carbon guns, and all kinds of scarecrows. The geese, though, were used to Oriental celebrations of all varieties and they *loved* the noise and the bizarre figures! We strung tin cans for miles to deflect the rays of the sun, hoping thereby to scare the birds away. Nothing had any lasting effect. As a matter of fact, the birds were attracted by the guns: whenever they heard them popping they knew it was dinnertime.

When finally the geese had just about cleaned us out, the rains came. The expression The Wet for the Australian rainy season is a deceptively simple description. They should call it The Deluge or maybe The Nightmare. We had known, of course, that the monsoon winds would bring up to sixty-five inches of rain during the three-month season. What we did not know is how that water would be distributed during that period. As it turned out, much of it came at one time. Drainage ditches and dikes which had been engineered to handle sixty-five inches of water if it fell more or less regularly throughout the three-month period were unable to hold fifteen inches in two days. And that is what we got in March of 1956. The rain did not come down in buckets; it came down in acre feet. The entire alluvial delta was one gigantic, devastating, all-encompassing lake. And by the time the skies had cleared and the water had drained away, there wasn't much left of our precious rice crop.

In spite of this disaster, we gave no thought to abandoning the project. We had too much money invested in equipment

Rice!!! Divebombing geese approaching target.

From The Dry to The Wet—a desert can become a lake in seconds.

and the ground preparation to give up so quickly. We had learned a lot (the hard way, to be sure) but what we learned, we were certain, would stand us in good stead in the years to come. Fortunately, the rice that managed to survive the flood turned out to be of excellent quality and yielded abundantly. All we had to do, it seemed to us, was build stronger dams, buy bigger pumps, detour the geese to New Zealand, plant again, and our troubles would be over. We knew our enemies; now it was simply a question of devising weapons to overcome them.

We engaged one of the top engineering firms of Australia to design a system for controlling the heavy rains. They surveyed the terrain and laid out a network of levees and dikes calculated to contain not only the monsoon rains from the hills, but the thirty-five-foot tides which swept up and down the Alligator River from the sea. We ordered the most up-to-date pumps brought all the way across Australia from Sydney to handle the excess water. Roads would be laid on the top of the levees to permit easy access to the rice paddies during the wet season. Great tractors were imported to disc the ground and prepare the seedbeds. We planned to increase the acres planted to ten thousand, which would bring forth a million-dollar crop.

With all this going for us, I felt that we were well on the way toward our goal. And as I left to return home, I must say everything looked promising in spite of the difficulties. The next trip would certainly be different.

I was right. The next trip *was* different. It was *worse!*

CHAPTER FOUR

Après Moi, le Déluge or It Rained Again—Like Hell

The day I got back to Hollywood after our first experience with rice-growing, I passed by Sam, my favorite news dealer, at his stand on the corner of Hollywood and Vine. He knew about my adventures down under, and had, in fact, offered to become an associate if forty bucks would buy into the deal.

"Did you see a crocodile down under?" he asked right away. "And how about that platypus—does he really lay eggs?"

I told him that I had seen one crocodile at a careful distance on a mud bank, but nary a platypus. He seemed disappointed. "However," I assured him, "we laid a big egg ourselves at Humpty Doo."

"They tell me there's a lot of our California eucalyptus in Australia," he countered hopefully. I was glad to change the subject. My chest swelled with the pride of knowledge as I carefully pointed out to my friend that it was just the other way around. "The eucalyptus is only one of the many arboreal gifts Australia has made to other arid and tree-hungry areas of the world. Magnificent stands of eucalyptus trees, all from Australia originally, are now found in Russia, Ethiopia, Italy, and many parts of South America. The eucalyptus is so adaptable, it can live in Australia's bone-dry desert or at snow level in the mountains of the East."

It was clear to me that Sam was impressed by my fund of knowledge. Having a captive audience (one of my greatest pleasures in life) I went on. "Most interesting of the Australian trees, though, is the grotesque bottle tree, or baobab. Its silver-gray trunk has the feel and color of human skin, and when seen across the arid plains of the northwest, it looks like a monstrous demijohn standing like a welcome pub in the desert. And there is more to this resemblance to a whiskey jug. These great bottle trees, and some of them are twenty feet in diameter, contain fresh water that can be tapped at the base of the branches. The tiny branches of foliage sprout from the top of the baobab like a tuft of sparse hair on a bald man's head; but in the spring the trees clothe themselves with magnificent, fragrant yellow blossoms resembling cactus blooms. This freak of nature produces a sap that is eaten by the aborigines. And from time to time the hollowed-out trunks of these great turnip-like growths have been used by northwest policemen as temporary jails for cattle rustlers and other lawbreakers."

"How about that!" Sam interrupted, "I hear the broads are terrific, and the beer real potent . . ." I left Sam in midsentence since my Australian research had been supervised by my wife and definitely did *not* include that kind of fauna.

For quite a while after I returned to Hollywood, we kept getting reports from Humpty Doo saying the work was progressing well. First the dikes and levees were completed, then the pumps were installed, and finally the seed was sown. And when word of the first rains came we felt secure, like the third of the three little pigs in his brick house.

The summer that followed our third planting set an all-time record for rain. The water came. And came. And came, and it kept coming. It came down in torrents, overflowing its channels and washing away or drowning everything in its course. Our new and expensive pumps labored valiantly and our crews worked around the clock trying to stem the flood. Then one by one, as the dikes washed out and the flood did not abate, the pumps blew up or ran down or burned up or were drowned. First, new parts and then whole new pumps were flown in but

The "Bottle" tree. Pioneer: *"Didn't ANYONE bring an opener?"*

there was no place to put them down. Project Marco Polo was a pathetic, water-drenched sea of disaster. Seedbeds were under as much as five feet of water which drowned the young rice plants. Our levee roads were hopelessly blocked with deeply mired tractors, land-rovers, and jeeps. And when at last the titanic monsoon flood slowly abated, draining off as it had for millions of years into the Arafura Sea, what had been our precious, costly seedbeds were muddy lakes.

Even so, it was not a complete fiasco. Here and there a dike had held and several of the pumps had survived. Here and there a few acres of rice popped out of the mire. The whole survival kit added up to only a few hundred acres—a twentieth of what we had planted.

After the water had done all the damage it could, we had to concentrate on keeping the birds from eating the plants that had managed to survive. At a minimum, we hoped to salvage a few pounds of seed for the next planting. The special carbon guns were reactivated and went off with a loud boom every three minutes; and long strings of flashing objects which whirled in the wind were raised, to be given a tug every now and then by a passing workman. But as we overcame one obstacle another popped up.

One enemy we hadn't taken into consideration was the water buffalo. Tens of thousands of these beasts graze the Top End as American buffalo used to graze the central plains. They can smell young green plants for miles downwind, and a herd of them came into our area, uprooted the few feeble fences we had built and mercilessly trampled the tender rice plants.

Another hazard, while not a threat to our crops, was the twenty-foot-long, seagoing, nonvegetarian marine crocodile which would swim up the flooded Alligator River on a foraging expedition, seeking particularly, it seemed, that succulent meat that walks around on two legs. To my knowledge, the crocs didn't snare a victim, but it made it a little difficult to get workmen to slosh around in the flooded fields.

Through it all, the Hollywood Pioneers kept up a brave

Crocodile hunters.

front, as pioneers must. With each new misfortune we sent new money; with each new crisis we sent another expert; anything to put Humpty Doo back together again.

Then, when everything that could be salvaged appeared to be growing as promised and we seemed to be on our way to a record crop per acre, The Dry came. Like The Wet, it is a succinct, pithy name, laconic and to the point, but it does not come close to describing the withering, abysmal, devitalizing, soul-searing heat which descends upon this part of the outer outback, at the top of the land down under.

We were to learn that during The Dry the temperature never dropped below 90, day or night, and that in the direct rays of the humid sun the thermometer climbed to a broiling 120 degrees. The land which would be so green and fertile from March through May would become so parched during The Dry that any growing plant would wither and die or go into suspension. The river became a trickle, and great cracks checkerboarded the earth's black crust as the dizzying sun sucked the last bit of moisture from the soil.

Now the hungry geese were long gone, the water buffalo had retreated to other feeding grounds, and the Alligator River, which in the rainy season had done so much damage, became brackish from the saltwater which invaded the land for forty miles.

But despite everything, we did harvest a crop of rice. Not anywhere near as much per acre as we had hoped, but what we did harvest was excellent—in fact, superb—quality; and that gave us at least a little satisfaction. Our faith in Project Marco Polo had been badly shaken, but all the disappointments notwithstanding, we were still not ready to give up. We took refuge in a blend of wounded pride and martyrdom. We weren't cowards. We could not quit. If we could do what we had set out to do, it would be good for Darwin and the surrounding area, it would be good for Australia and the world, and, we still hoped, it would be good for us.

The history of the world is full of stories about men who faced and conquered insuperable obstacles. We kept telling

The Wet.

The Dry.

ourselves that danger and opportunity go hand in hand, that Hannibal did not quit when he faced the Alps with his army of elephants, that Washington did not quit when he and his men were freezing and starving at Valley Forge, and that Daniel did not quit when he was thrown into the den of lions. Maybe the truth is that they were as dumb as we were. But we tried again.

Our fearless leader, Allen Chase, who would not have been deterred if the entire continent had upended, was of the opinion we had not "thought big enough." In his estimation we had been trying to do a gigantic job in a picayune way. What we needed, he decided, was a new partner with imagination, courage, and, not least, lots of money. So Allen went out and found him.

Even in Los Angeles, filled as it is with bold and daring entrepreneurs, Robert McCullough stands out. He wrote the book on unconventionality. An international leader in the small-motor field, he pioneered the portable, motorized saw and chewed out a fortune. He put together a thriving oil-drilling syndicate. In fact, almost everything he has touched, to put it to Yankee music, has turned to gold. A swinger when it comes to betting on his business hunches, he envisioned, for example, a new city in the Arizona desert called Havasu, now a thriving community on a bank of the Colorado River near Parker Dam.

When the fantastic story of Project Marco Polo was relayed to McCullough he heard the same distant drums we Pioneers had heard three years before. He selected two of his trusted aides and sent them down under to see whether Humpty Doo was a busted egg or a substantial and fertile proposition. The men he chose were hardheaded pragmatists who knew that if they recommended the project to their boss the chances were he would dump it smack into their laps. And that's exactly what happened.

These two gentlemen spent a couple of weeks at Humpty Doo and Darwin, and when they returned from the heat and the dust and the dismal record of defeat that had been written

The Dry. Seaman: *"Just time for one up at the pub while we're waiting for the tide."*

The Wet. Golfer: *"I've found the ball—now we'd better camp here 'til someone finds us!"*

by the monsoons, the buffalo, the geese, and The Dry along the Alligator River, who would have guessed that they would be so enthusiastic as to recommend that Bob McCullough back our play? But that's just what they did! Indeed, the bottom line of their report actually urged Bob to take over the entire operation and give us Pioneers what amounted to an override on the net profits for the money we had expended.

For four years we Babes-in-the-Hollywood had fought nature, prayed for the breaks, and poured in the greenbacks—to little avail. And now Bob McCullough seized the torch and ran with it.

Nothing would please me more than to report that he was successful, but unhappily it didn't work out that way. He retained Bill Gunn and Bill faithfully repeated for his new client many of our original mistakes. Today the rusted hulks of ploughs, abandoned tractors, and milling machinery stand as mute testimony to the failure of Project Marco Polo and to the primordial, erosive power of the monsoon rains, the devastating heat, and the untamed ferocity of the Top End.

Though we Pioneers are still discussed derisively in the pubs along Main Street in Darwin, a handful of Australian farmers do grow small plots of rice in the area. And the fact that we failed in no way precludes eventual success in such an undertaking at Humpty Doo. Someday, when the government itself or some wealthy syndicate with a lot more money than we had builds the huge dams needed to control the seasonal floods and conserve the excess water for The Dry, this vast delta of rich farmland can truly feed much of mankind. Everything is there; the conducive climate, the water, the soil, and the Asian marketplace. And one day, you mark my words, Humpty Doo will come into its own.

But one good thing did come out of the disaster at Humpty Doo. We Americans learned a lesson that was to prove invaluable in our next Australian adventure: *Pick an area where you can control your problems economically and then move out from strength to conquer the land around you!*

By the time we were ready to leave Darwin and the Top

End, more than two million dollars* had gone down the drain. We had given it a "good go." We had hired the most experienced local management we could find, had engaged the best engineering firms, and had consulted the most highly respected experts. Certainly the men who worked for us, both Caucasian and aborigine, had tried their best to do the job. But even as giants could not dam the Colorado River out of the Salton Sea with a thousand sacks of cement, so we could not control, with our puny dams and pumps, the ocean of water brought on by the monsoon rains.

However, as the fellow says, it is an ill wind that blows everybody bad. And in the months of desperate search for a solution to our Humpty Doo dilemma, we made a discovery that was to change my life and the lives of many thousands of others. We came to love Australia and its people, and to learn that it truly is the land of opportunity. So long as you are not a quitter, so long as you have the faith to get up again and give it another go, the land down under is rich in the rewards of profit and accomplishment.

As word spread that we were forced to abandon the rice project at Humpty Doo, all kinds of propositions came to the Pioneers, urging us to "have another go." Cotton was being grown in New South Wales. A great dam was being planned for the Ord River which would change the face of northwestern Australia. There were rumors of vast mineral resources in Western Australia which tempted us until we learned they would require "about fifty million dollars" for railroads, ports, and machinery. Such a sum was slightly beyond our means. The federal goverment was planning new beef roads which would enable cattlemen to haul their live beef to market and get better prices for prime young stuff, so we considered going into the cattle business. Resort developers along the coast of Queensland thought we should invest in new hotels and recreation areas for the growing tourist business. And there were a few very wild-eyed dreamers, including Allen Chase, who thought that the expansive sandy plains of Esperance, five hundred miles southeast of Perth in Western Australia, could

* U.S. currency.

be developed into lush green Eden pasture for sheep. Vandeburg was right. Marco Polo fever is incurable.

Somehow, the Esperance proposition was most intriguing. Why, only the good Lord knows. The indefatigable Allen Chase had set about forming a new syndicate called the Esperance Plains Company. The syndicate had contracted to buy 1.5 million acres from the Australian Government and I decided to take 10,000 of them off his hands. I agreed to pay per acre only as much as Allen's group had paid the Australian Government—55¢. Even at 55¢, 10,000 acres represented $5,500, a considerable sum to toss away on land I'd never seen. But, I figured that 10,000 acres of land not under water was worth that risk. I'd had enough water for the time being.

The Esperance venture was a challenge, to say the least. Nothing like controlled pasture had been seriously tried on its scrub-dotted, bleak, treeless sandy plain. The soil was supposedly infertile. Roads were almost nonexistent. And as everyone knew, other efforts to settle Esperance had repeatedly failed. It seems fitting, therefore, that we thrice-cursed Babes-from-Hollywood should select this choice "dry lake" prospect for our next misadventure in the outback.

You say we were nuts? Don't be ridiculous. "Madmen" is a better word. But it is a truism that often the best place is where the crowd thinks otherwise. And measured by this yardstick, Esperance fitted the maxim to perfection. In any case the switch from the Top End to the Bottom End put a lot of distance between our failures.

Before we Pioneers left Humpty Doo for the 2,500-mile flight to Esperance, we put on old clothes, old boots, and mosquito netting, and went out for a farewell shuffle through the dust and rust of the punctured rice-bowl dream. It was a sad moment. Standing in the rich black soil with the subcoastal plain stretching off into infinity, I felt the wistfulness that comes to one who has done his best in a place, even without success, and is leaving it never to return. Despite the failure, part of my life and a lot of my dollars had gone down the tubes here, and now many of the might-have-beens, the should-haves and would-haves and if-onlys, went through my mind. I left the others and went into one of the virgin storage granaries we had built. There I salvaged a handful of spilled rice to take away with me as a souvenir of our wasted efforts. I threw a last rock at a lurking crocodile, still waiting greedily on the banks of the river, and waved good-bye to a half dozen of a new generation of geese that had flown in for their evening meal. It had been a rough go. But now we were ready to move on and make it all back in the place called Esperance, a French word for "hope," which does, indeed, spring eternal.

CHAPTER FIVE

People ARE Funny! And I Mean Me!

As we flew southwest from Darwin in an old, beat-up DC-3, heat waves rose in zigzag mirages from the dry soil the Australians call "bull dust." Patches of gray salt bush dotted the scape like pebbles dropped on a beach. There was a lunar gloom and lifelessness about the wilderness that gave me the uneasy feeling it was not yet a place for people. The termite mounds looked more than ever like monuments to lost souls.

If man feels somewhat lost and unwanted on the outer spaces of Australia, it is because three quarters of its surface is made up of pre-Cambrian rock, dating to a time and place before man-sustaining land existed. To give you a vivid idea of how deep in time that was, Australia had long since settled into her changeless shape when the Rocky Mountains, the Himalayas, the Andes, and the Alps were bulging into birth. Australia's mountains, now worn down to stubs by myriad rains and wind erosion, were once as colossal as the highest peaks of the Himalayas. Today by comparison, they are nothing but hills.

We were in a DC-3 operated by the MacRobertson-Miller Airlines, affectionately known throughout the land as the Mickey Mouse Airlines—"Bring Your Own Cheese." The tag line was added by my ever-hungry partner, Vandeburg. Its

Art Linkletter meets the DC-3: *"In THAT?!!"*

planes will land at any cattle station to deliver people, freight, or medicine. For such unscheduled stops the charge is eighty dollars. They carry everything imaginable—serum, tools, spare parts, refrigerators, chickens, beer, and whiskey. Airplanes in Australia are considered in the nature of marsupials; they enpouch everything of importance. In fact, everything in Australia seems to come in a pouch, including some mail and maybe including babies.

There are several ways to get about in Western Australia's Top End; by jeep or utility truck—known as a ute—by coastal ship, on horse or camel back and on foot, depending on the season and the distance to be traveled. The use of camels for freight transportation today is less frequent than in the past. People don't ride horses so much anymore, either, except for mustering cattle where the jeeps cannot go and, of course, for racing anywhere on any provocation.

Planes are particularly important for the transportation of doctors and dentists, prize rams and pregnant outback wives.

Not necessarily, but realistically, in that order. The arrival of a plane on a passenger stop in the outback is heralded by whirls of red dust zeroing in from all directions to the landing place. These whirls are stirred up by the cars of people who have heard the radio announcement of the plane's arrival. Some come to pick up freight or to meet passengers; others come just to satisfy their hunger to see other human beings.

The word "outback" describes the vast and rugged unsettled regions of Australia, the terminology of which is often contradictory. For example, when an Aussie goes to the settled urban areas of Australia, he is going "outside"; and when a resident of the outback is going to town, which is most likely to be on the coast, he will also say he is going "outside." The most rugged and remote regions of the outback are referred to as back-of-beyond.

The western third of Australia, which has an area as great as a third of the continental United States without Alaska, has a population of around 835,570, most of which is concentrated in the southwestern region around Perth. It is a lonesome land parched for water and hungering for people, skills, and fertilizer.

In the outback those who like to play golf and participate in other sports often use the airstrip for a playing field. As a rule, it is the only ground that is level and cleared of stones, termite mounds, and scrub. On Koonlan Island, where there is a big iron ore operation, the airstrip is the only surface that doesn't have a sharp slope, and this serves as what is probably the world's longest golf hole—866 yards, a par seven. It is also the only hole on the course! There are those confirmed golfers who play the game even during The Wet, when the rough grows as much as ten feet high. The problem then is not only losing one's ball but losing one's partners. Conversely, during The Dry, hazards include lizards and snakes which mistake golf balls for bird's eggs and swallow them. At Port Hedland the airstrip is used as a rugby field. No matter what game is being played on these runways, the rule book states that all players must clear the field when they see an approaching pilot lower

Airstrip playing field. Footballer: "Better kick it, he's got his wheels down!"

his landing gear. And they may return to the field only after the takeoff dust has cleared.

Although the stewardess always announces for the benefit of public relations that the plane will be on the ground for "twenty minutes," the human relations ground time will range anywhere from twenty minutes to two hours, depending on the crew's ability to unload and find the desired item of cargo. Loading the planes is not always done systematically and there are times when the plane's entire contents must be disgorged before the necessary object to be delivered is found. Nobody protests these delays because, for one thing, impatience is futile in the outback and, for another, protesting doesn't do any good.

It was midafternoon and hot when the pilot picked out a bare salt pan on the parched earth and put the plane's wheels down. If there were any golfers, I did not see them. Bouncing over the rough runway, the DC-3 came to a stop with that sigh of frustrated exhaustion all planes exhale. I got out to stretch my legs but did not venture from the shade of a wing. Watching other perspiring passengers gather under the wing-space, I paraphrased Noel Coward: "Mad dogs and Englishmen may go out in the midday sun, but not Australians."

As the crew started pulling the cargo out of the marsupial pouch, several cars came dust-pluming toward us over that flatland which reaches to the Indian Ocean and inward to desert infinity. One of them was a station wagon. It came to a fast, tire-squealing stop and the driver, all urgency, popped out. In the back seat was a pale young man whose expression made it obvious he was in great pain. It developed that three of his fingers had been chewed off by a machine. What he desperately needed was a doctor.

The M.M.A. pilot, a long, lean lad with a slight growth of blond beard, came over, examined the wound, then turned to ask if there was a doctor among the passengers. Unfortunately, there wasn't, so the pilot returned to his cockpit and we heard him speaking into his radio microphone. Presently he came out again and said, "Ladies and gentlemen, the young man has been hurt and has a bad infection. His life may depend on us finding a doctor. I have radioed for one. If he can come and take care of him, we'll leave the boy here. If not, this plane will take him back to Broome. I hope none of you has any objection."

Returning to Broome meant 348 bumpy air miles. No one said a word, but as the pilot returned to the task of unloading the cargo the passengers applauded him.

This was one of my first experiences with the Australian's fierce sense of "mateship," or brotherhood—the determination to help his fellows. It is a pronounced part of the national character and has become ingrained in the Aussies because, I think, of the vastness of the land, the lack of communication, and the isolation. It is simply a matter of self-preservation. You help a man when he needs it, and when your turn comes, he will help you. Do unto others is still an essential way of life out there even if it seems in danger of becoming a casualty of civilization in America.

We had been en route from Darwin for what seemed like thirty years, but in truth was only about twenty stops and thirteen hours. But thank God for the airplane; over the miserable Great Northern Highway by car, it could have taken a week or two, depending on whether the unbridged rivers were "up" or "down" and on the seasonal state of the "washboard" surface that can shake a vehicle to pieces.

After flying for hours over low ranges, shallow boulder-filled gullies, and great expanses of flatland, it was a relief to see Perth's multistoried buildings rising jaggedly against the 230-foot "Mount" Eliza. Perth is a charming place, lying on both sides of the meandering Swan River. Built-up areas extend all the way to its harbor city, Fremantle, Australia's westernmost port. Adelaide, the closest city of any comparable size, is 1,700 miles away. Of all the cities I know, Perth most closely resembles San Diego in size, environment, and climate.

With a population of 400,000, Perth is the lovely outpost of civilization on the shore of the Indian Ocean that chose to turn on every light in the city as a beacon for our first astronauts as they orbited the earth. It is a place of English charm and Australian vitality, where English conservatism is nicely balanced with Australian muscle and forthrightness. With its polished brass hardware on its front doors and its wrought-iron fences, it is perhaps the loveliest city in Australia.

When we landed at Perth we were still 500 miles from Esperance and the 1.5 million acres of virgin land Chase had contracted to develop. We were so tired we decided to stop at Perth's famous Esplanade Hotel for a rest. Architecturally, the Esplanade is one of the world's charming small hotels, and its accommodations, food, and service are all first class. Furthermore, it is elegantly chandeliered, wood-paneled, carpeted, and as comfortable as an old kimono. And the lady who runs it is a character who should have a chapter all to herself.

When I went into the hotel lounge for a spot of tea, the room was beginning to fill with lady shoppers. Perth's women tend to be more formally dressed than their American counterparts. Those around me wore gloves that reached almost to their elbows, and a stunning array of feathered and flowered hats. Because of this formality, I was surprised that instead of tea, most of them ordered beer. At almost every table where several ladies were gathered, a large pitcher of suds was served up. I learned to take this for granted, because beer, rather than tea or coffee, is the Australian national drink, and women imbibe it almost as readily as men.

It was in Perth that I was made more aware of the Australian's scorn of material success. I think it is fair to say that most Australians resent any man who gets economically too far ahead of his neighbors. They believe that anyone has a right to riches if he earns them, but cleverness in money matters is considered un-Australian. A good example of this characteristic is an Australian who discovered a mountain of five million tons of high-grade iron ore in Western Australia. You would think that such discovery would have made him a national hero, because it immeasurably enhanced his country's economy. But he is not a hero among his prospecting mates. If he had found the ore and then given it away for the price of a few drunken sprees, he probably would have enjoyed the esteem of his outback friends. Instead, this prospector proved to be a hardheaded negotiator and a knowledgeable businessman. As a result, he became very rich. Over the next few years, it is estimated that he will receive several million dollars. As a grubstaked underdog, he was popular; as a self-sustained, wealthy overdog, he committed the un-Australian sin of becoming too rich.

After a two-day rest stop in Perth, we flew the four hundred miles southeast along the coastal bulge to our destination—Esperance, whose title, "city of hope," would be tested, almost disproved.

CHAPTER SIX

Esperance . . . Did You Say That Means Hope?

As we came in from the coastline, I had my first view of Esperance from ten thousand feet. Seeing it for the first time I contemplated asking the stewardess for an airsick bag. My queasiness came not from turbulence in the air but from the forbidding character of the land. Away from the coast, it is an expanse of dismal, gray-brown soil pockmarked with what proved to be salt pans. Nowhere was there a splash of pasture green, and a strong wind was blowing dry, fine grit called bull dust over the bleak landscape.

As soon as we landed, Lois and I got into a land-rover with a guide for the long drive inland to Condingup Mountain. Actually, Condingup is but a hillock, rising 250 feet above the level of the plain, but it is the highest point in these parts. The word "Condingup" is aborigine. It means camping place, and in aborigine the suffix *up* always denotes water.

I was eager to see the land that was to be the scene of our next Australian saga. I had done some homework as usual and had learned that in 1949 the Australian Government established an agricultural station at Esperance to determine what, if anything, could be grown there. The agronomists working at the station discovered that with the addition of superphosphate and the trace elements copper and zinc, the land could

Esperance, a coastal view.

be made to grow clover, rye grass, and other pasture plants.

To substantiate these findings, our investment group had sent Dr. Morton Love, of the University of California agricultural extension at Davis, to Esperance, and this distinguished farmer-scientist verified the findings of the research station. It was his opinion that with the addition of copper, zinc, and phosphate, luxuriant stands of cultivated grasses and clover could be raised to support, without supplemental feeding, two and perhaps three sheep per acre. Dr. Love ventured the opinion that the land itself could be easily and cheaply prepared for sowing because almost no trees existed on it, and the low bushes, scrub, and plants that dotted the plain could be quickly chained, dragged, and burned.

It was on the strength of Dr. Love's glowing report that I had contracted with Allen for the ten thousand acres.

In a very real sense, I was doing Allen a favor in buying the land from him. He had bitten off a big chunk to chew in a million and a half acres, and he needed help. For one thing, he needed publicity which would attract buyers and he thought my interest would have some value in this area.

As it turned out, he didn't need any help publicity-wise; he got more of this commodity than he had hoped for.

As we drove over the sandy, scrub-scattered flatland—so flat as to appear absolutely endless—our driver filled us in on the local lore. He told us about the 1891 gold strike at Coolgardie, a few miles to the north, and of the 160 million ounces of gold that had been taken from the mines there. In those days Esperance was a very busy place. He seemed to want to emphasize that point, as if to apologize for the town's present ghostlike appearance. During those exciting days, most of the argonauts who sought the golden fleece came from Perth by ship, the sea approach being far easier than the rigorous journey over land. Because of its fine harbor, Esperance became an important way station on the road to the mines in the inland desert. Hundreds of prospectors arrived on every ship and along with them came hundreds of cattle to supply food for the hungry miners. Since there was no jetty, the animals were

Allen Chase shows Linkletter's Condingup holdings: *"There you are, Art! That's ALL YOURS!!!"*

pushed overboard to swim ashore. Attacks by sharks were frequent, the driver said, and many of the steers reached the beach with great chunks of meat torn from their flanks.

"Arthur," Lois said, during a pause in our guide's monologue, "I've become resigned to your investing in Australia, but may I ask a question? Why do you want to buy land way out here? How about Sydney for a change?"

Now I like to visualize myself as being a person whose motivations are altogether logical and straightforward. I like to think that whatever I do, I do for a good and specific reason. But the truth is, at that moment I just didn't know what to say. Of course, I tried.

"I kind of thought I'd like to found a kingdom," I said to Lois as we jostled and bumped over the wide open flatland. "You know, like Tony Carlton." I was referring to a man, long since dead, who went to Italy, married an Italian girl, and was knighted for something or other by the King. It so happened, coincidentally, that he had inherited a considerable plot of land in New Mexico, so when the Italian King conferred the knighthood, he became known as Count of Mesa Verde. I had always thought this story was pretty exciting and romantic. "Maybe the Queen of England will knight me the Duke of Condingup," I threw in candidly.

Lois was not amused. She said, "Well, I certainly can't see us running down here for a weekend."

"Look, my love," I said, "you know I like to try things, and occasionally even to accomplish things. I don't always know exactly what the ultimate goal is going to be, but you wouldn't have me stop thinking ahead just because I have a lot of things going already, would you? Imagine what life would be like just resting on the beach!"

"You'd probably live longer," she said sardonically.

I tried to bolster my sagging spirits as we drove along by envisioning multitudes of nice fat sheep grazing in the fields, silos bursting with wheat and barley, and windmills pumping fresh, sweet water into reservoirs. It was a noble effort, but somehow that delightful picture appeared woefully out of focus when double-exposed on the harsh reality of the desolation which stretched before us as far as our eyes could see.

We finally came to the scrub-choked summit of Condingup and the driver braked the car. In every direction, the land fanned out like an ocean, and like an ocean it rippled on and on until it disappeared beyond the horizon.

"That's your acreage out there," our guide said, gesturing vaguely to the southeast.

As I looked out over that vast, empty, treeless space, it would have been impossible for me to put my feelings into words. I guess the word for it was "depressing." It did not take an agronomist to know that it would require Herculean effort and an enormous amount of money to bring that soil under cultivation.

I guess as a kid I read too many of the Horatio Alger, Jr., books, because I don't like to turn back or give up on anything. But at that moment, I must confess, I was sorely tempted to tell Mr. Alger's ghost to go to hell. We were sixty miles and three hours by bumpy dirt road from Esperance; there wasn't a lake, a stream, or any topographical relief whatever—there was just nothing but flat sandy land.

I tried not to let my despair show, but it wasn't easy. Lois took my hand and said, "Well, you always like a challenge!" She was kind enough not to spell it out, but I knew she was thinking of our disastrous experience at Humpty Doo.

"Are you *sure* you want to go on with this?" she ventured in a last plea. "There's no backing out now," I said, "I've given Allen my word. Besides, I'm about the last Apache left from the tribe of Hollywood Pioneers." Lois' look was the last word in that discussion.

Until the arrival of our remnant group of Hollywood Pioneers, the history of agriculture in Esperance was positively negative. Mostly there had been failures compounded by too few people trying to do too much with too little.

Historically, the first mention of agricultural possibilities at Esperance is dated January 10, 1802. A man by the name of Matthew Flinders visited Esperance and on that date he wrote in his journal: "The vegetation . . . consisted of an abundant variety of shrubs and small plants and yielded a delightful harvest to the botanist; but to the herdsman and the cultivator it promised nothing—not a blade of grass, nor a square yard of soil from which seed could be expected to take root."

In 1841 Edward John Eyre, who came to Esperance Bay, noted in his diary: "I accompanied the Captain [of the whaling ship *Mississippi*] to see a garden made by the sailors in which peas and potatoes had already been planted and appeared to be growing well. . . . I went with the Captain to visit an island where he kept his livestock, pigs and sheep and tortoises. The sheep were strange looking animals, more like goats than sheep, of all colors and with fat tails, like the Cape sheep. . . ."

Evidently that was the first farming ever done at Esperance and that is the first mention of sheep that I can find in the history of the town. A number of other agricultural efforts in the area were made on a larger scale over the intervening years, but one after another they failed until, in 1863, C. E. and H. Dempster acquired from the government a lease of 304,000 acres on which to graze sheep. Their leasehold lay mainly along the coast and it was the Dempsters and their helpers who laid the foundations for the settlement of Esperance.

The town sprang into importance twenty-eight years later, in 1891, following the discovery of gold at Coolgardie. It was the nearest port. More gold was discovered in the area two years later, and a deep-sea jetty was completed in 1897. The mines at Coolgardie alone have produced more gold than any other place on the face of the earth and some of the mines there are still in operation.

During those early gold-grubbing years at Esperance, the Royal Mail Coach would depart for Norseman every Tuesday and Saturday mornings at seven o'clock—a distance of 126 miles. The journey was made in three days and the fare was five pounds, or today ten dollars. Between Esperance and Norseman there were four principal stopping places where water and other potables were available. Thirsts were quenched at Gibson's Soak, Grass Patch, Salmon Gums, and Gilmore's Lake View. Also along the route there were nine saltwater conversion plants, spaced specifically to cater to the beasts of burden, mostly camels and horses.

At that time no effort had been made to sink deep wells or build dams, and water condensed from brackish surface pools was almost the only source of supply. The conversion method involved boiling the saline water in great tanks, and the steam created was carried off in galvanized pipes which condensed it into potable water. The freight was drawn by camels or horses at a cost of from £18 to £35 a ton (about $36 to $70). As many as sixteen horses would pull one load. These conveyances carried no passengers, there were coaches for that purpose. Prospectors could load their swag bags aboard the freight wagons but they themselves were forced to walk. The freight wagons would average about fifteen miles a day, so the trip to Norseman took about ten days.

One early traveler who made the trip by coach wrote: "Ample provision is made for the wants of travelers along the way, but Mrs. Graham, of Gibson's Soak, makes the travel more than usually comfortable. Her well-laid table with fresh-cut salads and tempting new-laid eggs, being sufficient to create an appetite in the most austere ascetic." As if to prove that the modern motorist is not the first driver to endure traffic problems, he continues:

"Complaints have been made of the camel drivers on the road refusing to take their camels off the track when meeting horse teams. The horses are very frightened of camels and frequent cases of bolting have occurred. Freighters using horses complain that through fright their horses will not drink for as much as an entire day after meeting camels."

Camel teams and camel pack trains were seen in a more friendly light by another observer who lived in Esperance:

"A sight we loved to watch was the setting out of a camel train. Prince Alana, owner of hundreds of camels, rode an almost white camel which was richly dressed in brightly colored saddle cloths and wore many strings of colored beads around its neck. Its gorgeous apparel was second only to that of its master. He wore a brightly embroidered velvet and silk vest and a flowing white turban sash that took our breath away as he rode out of town at the head of the train."

Attempts to raise grains and pasture grasses at Esperance were not successful during these formative years, and because of these failures the chief inspector for the Western Australia Agricultural Bank expressed the opinion that the "whole poor sand-plain, with the exception of occasional swamps toward the south" were in no way suitable for agricultural development.

He made that statement in 1916, and it was accurate for the time. However, with the establishment of the Esperance Downs Research Station of Western Australia's Agricultural Department in the area, scientific methods were brought to bear for the first time. The patience of the scientists proved the potential fertility of the soil. Immediately a wave of optimism about the Esperance Plains swept the country. People all over Australia began pressuring the Department of Agriculture for acreage. But development was slow.

In June 1954, there were but thirty-six farmers with a total of approximately 20,000 acres of developed land. The reason there were so few farmers was most likely financial. While the land itself could be had in blocks of 2,500 acres at a very low price, a great deal of money was needed to develop it. Experience proved that those who took up land without sufficient development capital lost their original investment. What was obviously needed, if Esperance was to come into its own, was large-scale development by companies or syndicates with adequate working capital. That's when we Hollywood Pioneers, under the hypnotism of Allen Chase, came again into the Australian picture.

Allen's company was to clear, cultivate, and lay down pastures on half of the 1.5 million acres. The developed land would then be subdivided into blocks of 2,000 and sold to settlers. On each block the company agreed to build a house and provide fencing.

When news of this deal hit the headlines, excitement was generated not only in Western Australia but all over the continent. Extravagant forecasts were made and everybody wanted to get into the action.

U.S. PRESS WILL PUT ESPERANCE TO MILLIONS, the *West Australian* banner-lined the news. And Esperance buzzed with excitement as it found itself world famous. Optimism was everywhere. Business firms eager to get in at the beginning made inquiries as to the possibility of opening branches in the town. More pubs were opened. Ladies came to town. It was the gold rush all over again.

"The biggest agricultural land scheme ever undertaken by private enterprise in Australia is under way at Esperance, Western Australia, where American capital is preparing 1.5 million acres for subdivision into farm sites," one regional account read. "Twenty American millionaires under the leadership of Allen Chase of Los Angeles, have formed a syndicate which will pay about $800,000 for the land and then spend $35 million developing it. Under an agreement with the State Government, the first section of the vast area has been selected by the developing company. It is a tract of 60,000 acres east of Esperance. First ploughing is expected to begin in December."

The big adventure had re-begun—and once more I was one of the pioneers! I'm sure it was incurable optimists like me who prompted H. L. Mencken's barb: "Hope is a pathological belief in the occurrence of the impossible."

CHAPTER SEVEN

Fun and Games Chez Grace Darling

After jouncing over the sixty miles of corrugated dirt road to Condingup and back, Lois and I eased our wracked bodies from the land-rover in front of Esperance's one hotel, the Grace Darling. The Grace Darling is neither darling nor graceful, but after that torturous ride it was the Ritz and the Waldorf all wrapped up in one. And the sound and scent of the Indian Ocean gave us new life.

We rejoined our fellow travelers in the pub, figuring that was the best place to start the revival process. The crowded pub had a bare floor and a high ceiling. A small hole in the wall was the access to "self-service" beer. On another wall, providing action and a reason to lay bets, was a dart board. A dart board is to an Australian what an altar is to a church, and playing darts and drinking beer go together like the hands of a clock.

Outback Australian men are, for the most part, vertical drinkers. They don't sit down. During the legal drinking hours, called the swill, their saloons are always jam-packed with drinkers, animation, and raucous enjoyment. So it was in the pub of the Grace Darling. Many of the Aussies were newcomers to the town, some of them were blokes looking for an easy buck. There were stockmen from as far as four hundred

Outback hotel.

miles away, and there were workers from the gold fields at Coolgardie and Kalgoorlie. There were men off the fishing boats and drifters from down east, and then there were the farmers, the sheepmen, the drovers, and well drillers.

As the suds went down, so did the inhibitions, and it wasn't long before everybody in the place was slapping someone on the back and making like old friends. After a few beers and some of that fine, hearty Australian mateship, even I began to feel better, and our undertaking at Esperance gradually began to take on a rosy hue.

The drinking habits of Australians are a hangover from those brought from England by their ancestors. While Australians are zestful and inclined to be lusty lovers of life, there is a strong strain of puritanism in them. If an Aussie drinks, he does so with exuberance and gusto, but if he doesn't drink, he will likely frown on those who do. The puritanical influence is further indicated by the restricted legal drinking hours and by the fact that drinking is chiefly limited to beer and to bars in hotels. A typical country hotel may have only a few rooms, which aren't used much, but its bar will do a booming business. The hours during which bars can be open differ in the various states, but generally speaking they open at 11 A.M. and close no later than 10 P.M. In some towns the "beer off" bell rings for an all-male clientele at 6 P.M.,* so workers who leave their jobs at five or thereafter have very little time to tipple, and that hour before the bars close becomes a madhouse of rapid-fire elbow bending. Everyone wants to swill down all he can, and not only do they drink more than they should, they drink it too fast, usually on an empty stomach. Sometimes the results are dramatically explosive.

It would seem logical that Australians, being such lusty embracers of life, would abandon such typically English restrictions as the limited drinking hours, and maybe someday they will. The influx of immigrants since World War II is changing a lot of habits in food and drink.

People had poured into Esperance a few days before we arrived and the place was jumping. It was like it must have been

* Since changed.

Barmaid: *"Common mate! Make up ya bluddy mind! Whaddaya gunna have?!"*

during the gold rush of the 1890's, when, according to a lady who wrote of that time, "people were sleeping in the seaweed. The place is thronged with people making for the gold fields. Streets are poor with sand everywhere, and there are fleas by the millions. . . ."

To the natives, we Americans were objects of intense interest and not a little amusement. Some of those who flocked to Esperance came to "have a look at the Yanks." Aside from the Hollywood characters, a number of advisers—attorneys, accountants, and agronomists—had come with us from Perth, and I suppose we were an odd-looking crew. Some of us wore suits and ties, some jeans and open-necked shirts and our women wore slacks. Like so many American tourists, most of us wore dark glasses and had cameras hanging from our necks. Our combined appearance caused a considerable amount of comment.

One Australian newsman wrote of us: "They all looked the same to me. In fact, they looked like a group of oddly attired

"People are BLOODY Funny."

Englishmen. At least I learned one thing: you can't tell the difference in dress or speech between a millionaire and the one who just looks as if he wanted to be one."

In the Grace Darling pub we Americans were required by custom to take our turns at "shouting," which means we kept buying alternate rounds of drinks, and with every round the pace of the party increased. One of the Aussie ladies who looked somewhat like an overstuffed schoolteacher or librarian—not at all the betting type—challenged me to a game of darts. "Would you," she said sweetly, "play for a beer all around?"

I looked the thirsty mob over and said, "I hope your credit's good."

As we prepared to play, I was thinking I should take it easy with the lady; it would not be good sportsmanship or good public relations to beat her too badly. As things turned out, I should have reserved all of my sympathy for myself. The lady proceeded to skunk me with a bull's-eye accuracy that, as the fellow says, wouldn't quit. When it was all over and everybody was having a fresh glass of suds on me, she was formally introduced to me as the local champ.

Another game they play all over Australia in pubs and elsewhere is two-up. It may even be more popular than darts, and it comes as close as any sport, excluding beer-guzzling, to being the national pastime. The fact that it is illegal deters no one. Indeed, that is one of its several charms.

We all gathered in a circle in the Grace Darling pub, and one Aussie, who was somewhat larger than the others, elected himself "ringer," which means referee. Everyone would like to have this job, because for his services the ringer gets 10 percent of the bets. One player, called the spinner, was handed a small board on which had been placed two of the large English pennies. The head side of the coins had been burnished so that they were shining, while the tail sides had been left dull. Before the spinner tossed the coins we all made bets, one with another, on whether the pennies would fall heads or tails up. If one fell head and the other tail, they would be tossed again.

I was flabbergasted by the rapidity with which the bets were

Lady darts players in a pub.

Waitress: *"'Ands up all those that want soup."*

laid and the follow-through of the ringer calling for the spinner to toss the coins. The latter did this by holding his arm and the board at full length above his head and tossing the pennies so that they spun before hitting the floor.

The old English pennies are ideal for playing two-up, but now, with the coming of what the Aussies call "funny money," they have been replaced with coins smaller and lighter than the American cent. Australia changed her money in 1966 from the English sterling pound-and-pence to the decimal system dollars-and-cents. This created a multitude of problems, and millions in cost to effect an orderly changeover. Cash registers and coin machines had to be modified, and the entire country was thrown into monetary confusion. But affected worst of all, perhaps, was the game of two-up.

The new Australian penny bears Queen Elizabeth's likeness on the head side and a feather-tailed glider, Australia's smallest marsupial, on the other.

"It just isn't possible to play two-up with a feather-tailed glider," one of the gold miners recently said to me. "They float on you."

Nevertheless, though it may have put a crimp in the game of two-up, Operation Funny Money has been highly successful in Australia. The Australian dollar is valued at about $1.11, U. S. (compared to the pound, which was then worth $2.25, U.S.). Shops were compelled to advertise items in pounds as well as dollars during the changeover period of eighteen months, but have now been requested by the government to advertise their prices in dollar currency only, though no law as yet enforces this ruling.

The changeover took three years to effect. All people who deal with public money, such as bank tellers and store clerks, took courses in handling the new monetary exchange. The largest bank in the nation gave thousands of seminars for the public. The telephone department had "dollar girls" to answer inquiries.

Reporting on the funny money, Richard F. McMillan wrote to the Los Angeles *Times:*

Bar customer to Hollywood Pioneer: *"Whaddaya doin' the next few days, mate? We're one shy on the fencin' team!"*

"There was the steady customer at a pub, who put aside his racing form long enough to study the conversion table. His eyes lit up as he discovered that if he bought one glass of beer it would cost him eleven new cents, but if he bought three glasses at a time, it would cost him thirty-two cents, a one-cent saving. He proceeded to do so, but by the time he had saved five cents he was in no condition to place his bets."

A Sydney cabbie told me he had just discharged an elderly lady who, when he told her the fare was seventy cents, asked, "How much is that in Australian money?"

"That is Australian money, lydy," replied the cabbie.

"I mean how much is it in real money?" she demanded.

"Seven shillings, lydy," the cabbie said in surrender.

One of Australia's most unusual outback pastimes is a man-to-man competition called Bull Fight that takes place in the pubs of the Northern Territory during the three months of The Wet, when there is nothing to do but drink and play cards and practical jokes. In Bull Fight, one man pits himself against another, not to display any particular skill but to prove toughness and courage or at least hardheadedness. After bets are placed, contestants get down on all fours and go at each other headfirst, butting skull to skull until one either concedes defeat or is knocked unconscious. The term "numbskull" may have originated here in a Top End Bull Fight.

George Johnston speaks of the Bull Fight in his excellent book *The Australians* and says that it offers Australians another opportunity to gamble. "It is at least a change from gambling on faraway race meetings, the fall of coins, the run of cards in a pack, the passage of two bull ants across a log or the color of a barmaid's underwear."

The Australians at Esperance looked upon us as a "weird mob" and seemed unable to believe we had come so far from the golden land of California to put money in their sand plains. They asked us innumerable searching and sometimes very personal questions, and we told them more than a few hopeful lies.

Well, I guess they weren't meant to be lies; they just turned out that way, being born of bravado and ignorance. The townspeople presented Allen a painting in appreciation for what he was about to do for their community. He gave them the impression, as indeed he did all of us, that the sleepy little town would eventually be turned into a thriving metropolis. But then, whatever Allen Chase believes is *fait accompli.* He predicted that within a few years Esperance would be the hub of a great wool industry. He announced that his syndicate was going to develop tens of thousands of acres of land into 640 farms for sale to the Australian settlers for cash or on terms. The possibility of buying land "on time" was especially good news, because generally banks were not interested in making loans to homesteaders in the area.

"And liberal terms they will be," I overheard Allen telling one young man. "We'll have forty thousand head of livestock pasturing on the sand plains within a very short time, you mark my words. We are going to grow four sheep to the acre out here and we're going to feed them the year around on permanent, fenced, cultivated pasture."

Others heard him say these words and they were quoted throughout the town. The statements were considered in the nature of broad extravagances, which at the time they were.

Sheep are insatiable grass-burners and raising three sheep to an acre of pasture is considered good production almost anywhere. Surprisingly enough, we eventually did raise four sheep to the acre in Esperance and the time is almost here when we'll be raising six or even eight to an acre on Linkletter's Place near Esperance. When that time comes, it will go down in the history of animal husbandry as something of a miracle.

CHAPTER EIGHT

I Got Stuck in the Clover

After what we told the people of Esperance and the newsmen, every newspaper in Australia came out with stories of our enterprise or, as Aussies say, "scheme." Allen Chase became as near being a hero as Australians could permit. He was photographed and interviewed, and we, his associates, were wined and dined and "shouted" to the point of hangover and indigestion. People who had never heard of Esperance became intrigued and headed west. Something approximating a Kansas land rush ensued. Overnight, Esperance seemed to grow from a sleepy village into a boom town. "Hope" and Esperance were once again synonymous.

The *Daily Telegraph,* in an article headlined GO WEST YOUNG MAN, reported: "There's a boom in Western Australia, but it doesn't spring from oil or gold. It comes from cheap land. And there's plenty of it. It is estimated that two million acres of land are available for development in assured rainfall areas where both crops and pastures can be grown."

Kirwan Ward, in his *Daily News* column, wrote: "These last few days Esperance has become a boom town. The bars, always barometers of prosperity, have been packed to the point where carrying three full glasses from one side of the room to the other is a considerable feat.

"Super highways, Hilton pubs, television shows—! I'm shootin' through before they ruin the joint!!"

"Farmers brought their wives in from such places as Circle Valley, Grass Patch, and Gibson's Soak. Salesmen from Perth drove in, their hats stained rust-red with dust. Newsmen were there from far-off magazines. The smell of excitement was in the roaring pubs and in the packed dining rooms where foaming glasses of beer were downed between big talk of the 'next ten years.'

"It was a stimulating thing to be there and to see Allen Chase and his party staring across their wide lands, the unmistakable gleam of excitement and adventure in their eyes. . . .

"The promise of Esperance is real and rich, and whatever the immediate outcome, there can't be the slightest doubt that the tremendous stimulus of American interest in the area must be beneficial. The thing to do, as I see it, is to view the picture calmly. . . ."

Not everyone in Australia did "view the picture calmly." Indeed, some Australians were of the opinion that, by making the land available to Americans, the Australian Government was cheating them of their birthright. One David Frith, in an article in *The Bulletin*, wrote of the Esperance development: "It is regrettable that Australians were never given a look-in on the ground floor. The scheme could have been financed with Australian capital, the land settled with Australian farmers and brought into production quicker that way."

Other Australians, however, came to our defense. They were quick to point out that the land at Esperance had been available for homesteading for half a century, and that the numerous underfinanced settlers who attempted to farm the land thereabouts had either failed or been able to make but a bare existence. There were a few exceptions to this—for example, William and Frank Kirwan, who had come here a few years before and through hard work and intelligent planning had developed a productive farm. But these men were exceptions. Where they managed to make a fair profit on the land, many, many others who ventured farther inland failed.

For nearly half a century the potential of this area had been known. Even as far back as 1912, Parliament had selected a

Aussie interrogates Allen Chase: *"You the Yank that threatened to turn this sleepy little town into a thriving metropolis?!"*

Chairman of Condingup hospitality committee: *"Rustle up some pickled python and a slab of damper, Blue—here come the Hollywood Pioneers!!"*

study committee which reported favorably on it. But if Allen Chase and the Hollywood Pioneers hadn't bet their shirts on a dream, it might have been another fifty years before anything was done with the land that we undertook to develop.

Actually, we didn't get the land so easily. There were obstacles. Before the government was able to negotiate the sale of the 1.5 million acres to our syndicate, the land act had to be amended by Parliament. Up until that time the government was not permitted to sell plots of land exceeding 5,000 acres. When the matter came up for debate in Parliament, there was considerable opposition; some members resented Americans trying to change Australian law and others openly admitted that they were afraid we might make big profits from the project. There was criticism of the looseness of the agreement between the Australian Government and the syndicate, and the Premier finally had to point out that since our company expected to spend upward of forty million dollars on the project, we had to be allowed a reasonable amount of latitude.

Despite the many agricultural failures over the years, Esperance has a temperate climate similar to the coastal belt of California from Santa Barbara to San Diego. It is almost entirely frost-free and the rainfall is more dependable than in other areas (an average of twenty-two inches annually). We found that once the land is properly conditioned, almost anything that can be grown in California can be grown at Esperance: flowers, varied fruits and vegetables, including avocados, strawberries, and citrus, and other Mediterranean crops. The secret, of course, was in adding—and continuing to add—the missing mineral trace elements and fertilizer to the hungry soil.

The syndicate decided to hire Australian William Gunn again as managing director of the Esperance operation and Australian R. R. Moule as general manager. Gunn had been at the helm when we went aground at Humpty Doo, and maybe it would have been wise to have dropped him overboard, a la Jonah, as bad luck; but no, we were loyal if nothing else. Part of the failure of Project Marco Polo had to fall on Gunn's shoulders, but we felt that his reported experience in animal husbandry would be of great value to us at Esperance. Moule's experience was also in the animal field rather than agriculture, which we thought we needed. It turned out that this was one of our biggest mistakes. Bill may have been great with animals, but to coin a pun, we were "jumping the Gunn."

You see, raising sheep was not really our *immediate* concern at Esperance, but rather our ultimate goal. The *first* mission was to prepare the soil and raise adequate pasture for the sheep. It should have been obvious that what we needed was a manager highly skilled in agronomy rather than animal husbandry. Sometimes you wonder how "smart" men can be so dumb.

I'm not sure exactly how the original approach to preparing the soil for pasture evolved, but I am inclined to put the finger on Dr. Jesse Skoss, an American agronomist whom Chase hired to oversee the practical work of plowing and seeding the land. I suspect him because, in a statement he made ten years later, he said: "One of the Australian Agriculture Department's recommendations with which I disagreed was the necessity of letting the plowed land lie fallow for two years. [The department actually estimated that it would take *five* years to bring the land up enough to support three sheep to an acre.] It was my belief that, within a year after beginning the work of root grubbing, burning, plowing, harrowing, and seeding, sufficient pasture could be produced to carry two and a half to three sheep to the acre. This entails perhaps the use of a little more fertilizer, more careful attention to the work of cleaning up the land, and the use of urea."

Well, you know how Americans are, speed and action are the name of the game. It was clear that Dr. Skoss acted in good faith; he was trying to save us money. And it can be said further in his defense that if the plowing had been more thorough, his theory might have worked out all right. Anyway, because he was saying what we wanted to hear, we went along with Dr. Skoss's recommendation and the whole routine of discing, fertilizing, and seeding was done in one stepped-up operation. Disaster compounded!

In December 1956, we signed a contract with the Esperance Construction Company to plow sixteen thousand acres, more

Project Marco Polo gets underway.

or less. I say more or less, because when we actually began to plow in the spring of 1957, the boundaries were whimsically indistinct. The survey lines were both erratic and poorly defined. In the face of such a vast expanse of raw land it was hard to tell where one man's boundary ended and another's began. It reminded me of a Spanish-Californian land grant which permitted a man to claim as much acreage as he could measure with a lariat while riding from sunup to sundown. The grant could be enormously increased by the claimant if he took a relay of fast horses and, as a token of measurement, merely dragged the rope behind. Incidentally, the metes and bounds of one such California grant were informal to say the least. The document says in part: "Southward to a lightning scarred oak upon a dry creek; thence westward to a rise of land whereat a buzzard roosts upon a yucca stump." It was kind of like that in those early days at Esperance. The government surveyors hadn't yet completed their work. The land lay flat as a lake and the newly formed Esperance Construction Company figured that plowing the land for seed would be a cinch, so they gave us a low, low economy price. The initial plowing was to be charged at eleven shillings an acre ($1) and the second plowing was to be nine shillings (90c) or a complete price of twenty shillings an acre ($2.00).

Now, everybody knows you get what you pay for, and that's what we got. We were the last to realize that the price we had been quoted and had accepted was too low to ensure a first-class job, and I suppose neither the contractor nor ourselves appreciated the difficulties of the task, particularly the nature of the country.

The contractor had a conglomerate of much-used tractors and to each of these were attached four 18-disc plows. They were spread out to cover an area of thirty-six feet and were to plow an average depth of four and one-half inches. The rigs were like a formation of side-by-side lawn mowers. They were also about as effective in penetrating the soil. In fact, the plows were spread out so far that if any of them had dug into the ground more than superficially, the tractor wouldn't have been able to pull them.

Anxious farmers in newly seeded field: *"Dammit, the stuff should be growing by NOW!!!"*

In our haste to get the soil prepared, we eliminated any clearing and burning of the brush, which would have taken several months. Theoretically, the disc plows were to grind up any such roots and rubbish and mix them into the soil.

For the initial plowing, Dr. Skoss selected about a thousand acres, then jumped a few miles to another section where the brush had been burned off accidentally. After that had been worked, and not very well, he brought the equipment onto what we all guessed was my land—none of us was sure—and plowed four square miles of it. This jumping about seemed necessary because in certain areas the vegetation was too dense and the brush stems too thick to plow in. Because we were in such a hurry, it seemed the thing to do to go around the tough acreage and plow somewhere else.

"It didn't take me long," Dr. Skoss said years later, "to realize that the entire effort was a poor one and that the program should be put back at least a full year and the plowing done all over again." Thus he admitted that due to the poor plowing job, his theory of saving time and money was unsound.

"I explained my conclusion to Mr. Gunn," Dr. Skoss said, "but he said that the plowing people had already been paid, that money for fertilizer and seed had already been spent, and that there wasn't sufficient money left to postpone the work for another year."

We, the landowners, were not consulted in this matter. In fact, the management of the work at Esperance in its early stages was very awkward. Bill Gunn was usually in Melbourne or Brisbane on strategic command business and had to get his information by phone from the Esperance front. His opinions were relayed to the board of directors thousands of miles away at subheadquarters in Perth. Their decisions were then phoned to Dr. Moule, on the beachhead at Esperance, and he would pass the instructions on to the man who was directing the plowing lines in the field. Finally, the word got down to Dr. Skoss who was tucked away somewhere in a bomb shelter!

In addition to the makeshift equipment the plowing contractor had hastily put together, the drivers were plucked from

Dauntless tractor operator: *"Ar, she'll be right, mate!"*

the very bottom of the Australian barrel. For the most part they were drifters, drawn to Esperance by the publicity, hoping to make a fast buck.

In the beginning, everyone was reasonably enthusiastic. The work was important to the future of Esperance and to all of Australia, and the drivers were being paid about £25 a week ($50). This was a high wage in Australia, though to earn it the men had to work twelve hours a day, seven days a week.

The work had not been under way very long, however, before the glamour had been worn off, for the drivers at least, by the dust, the heat, the breakdowns, and the obvious poor results of the discing. It is simply the nature of man, even a near derelict, to take some pride in whatever he does, and if the result of his effort is poor and he is powerless to improve it, he will become discouraged and resentful. That's exactly what happened at Esperance.

The work went on in two shifts—a pillar of dust by day and goldbricking by night. The cheating of some of the drivers on night shift was particularly flagrant. After making a few runs, some of the drivers would deliberately blow a tractor's light fuse or short the electrical system; anything so they would have an excuse to "sack out" by the tractor and not work. Some drivers didn't even go to that much trouble; they simply stopped their rig at the far end of a run and went to sleep. The plowing was always at least 25 percent behind the estimated progress, and the drivers became more and more careless.

Each investor had been assigned his own acreage and we were to pay for the plowing of our own individual plots. The problem was that we couldn't figure out for sure where our plots began and ended, and the drivers didn't worry much about keeping within even vague boundaries.

The carelessness of some of the drivers was unbelievable. Time and again halfway through a run, the feeding boxes on the tractors containing the superphosphate and the seed would empty and the drivers would just keep going on and on, putting absolutely nothing into the soil. Sometimes the trucks carrying the superphosphates to the tractors in the field got stuck in a bog and the driver would dump the precious sacks of phosphate under the rear wheels to get the truck moving again. Inoculin for the clover seed was shipped late and in too small a quantity. Boxes of this vital material were discovered under the bunk of the man whose responsibility it was to scatter it on the seed, and it had been there a whole month!

All these things, and many more, were costing each investor an enormous amount of money and it wasn't long before the situation became total chaos.

One of the main problems was that the machines which were used to plow and seed the pasture were sort of Rube Goldberg contraptions with outback accessories. Large discs prepared the furrows into which seeds, contained in seed boxes mounted above the discs, were sown. A platoon of little discs followed to cover the seed and a squad of rollers to compact the soil brought up the rear. As it turned out, the wiring was faulty and the sequence of events got out of kilter. The big discs fluffed the soil and the seed dropped into the furrow but the little discs didn't cover the seed and the rollers didn't compact the soil. Therefore, the seed lay naked in the open furrow, very quickly dried out, and failed to germinate. Moreover, I am personally convinced that the seed was planted upside down—and that isn't easy!

Rumor had it that every dollar we spent in Australia was costing us only ten cents in so-called hard money, and I have a feeling that this may have encouraged a few of the Australians who worked for us to place their personal profit motive slightly ahead of their characteristic honesty and integrity.

Another important factor that contributed to our first-year failure on the Esperance Plains was the weather. In the sixty years that weather records had been kept in the area, 1957 was the driest. Not a drop of moisture fell on our thirsty seed. Even our tears of dismay were salty and useless. Australian weather, always unpredictable, had plagued us in the rice paddies of Humpty Doo and here it was again in Esperance, but this time withholding the rain we so sorely needed.

CHAPTER NINE

Poor-boy's Heaven on Earth

The settled Australian farmers around Esperance watched our hasty, no-fallow operation with considerable interest and not a little skepticism. One of these was a young man who had recently graduated from an eastern agricultural college and, hearing that land could be had for a few shillings an acre at Esperance, had come on to poor-boy a homestead of his own. His name is John Hagon. He arrived about the time we did, and inasmuch as he is very much a part of my story, let us pause at this point, do a lap-dissolve, and bring him onto the Esperance-Linkletter stage.

John Hagon could very well be the basic reason for my success in Australia and for the continuity of my interest and faith in the land and its people. More than that, John Hagon is an outstanding example of how a young man anywhere may with drive, intelligence, and know-how reach the top.

Much of his determination and vision is reflected in the story of his homesteading trek to the west. More important, perhaps, is the fact that John Hagon today is a man of substance and importance in the Esperance community with land, livestock, and equipment worth at least $250,000.

John Hagon comes from a long line of Australian "doers." His grandfather was a mayor of Sydney. His father is a successful farmer in New South Wales, and John was born and brought up on his father's farm. In July 1956, which is the dead of winter down under, John went into Canowindra, the little town nearest his father's farm, to get spare parts for what he refers to as his "rather unreliable means of transport," his car.

John McCarran, the owner of the Canowindra garage, knew that John was yearning to have a farm of his own. So while he was helping John with his car, he gave some literature he had received from Perth that was designed to attract new settlers to the area around Esperance.

"This should be of interest to you, Youngblood," McCarran said. "There's cheap land out there if you can convince the government you have what it takes."

John Hagon studied the brochures with growing interest and excitement. His imagination was aroused. The land, he read, was level and with the proper additives could be made rich. The climate was superb—the best in Australia. It was a new frontier, and it beckoned with the same powerful magnetism that California exerted in the latter part of the nineteenth century. John Hagon said he immediately envisioned a farm just like his father's rich spread, "only with all the things just the way I personally would like to have them—healthy livestock, up-to-date equipment, and modern housing."

By the time he got home he was hooked. He read the literature to his father and mother who, as wise parents will, also became enthused with the possibility.

But let John tell the story:

I wrote to the Lands and Surveys Department in Perth for further details and waited anxiously for a reply. It is difficult to express my excitement. I wanted some of that land above anything else in the world.

When the letter came from the Lands and Surveys Department I opened it with mixed emotions—hopefully but with caution, preparing myself for disappointment. I need not have been so apprehensive. The envelope contained a questionnaire. I was to state my qualifications—age, educa-

tion, marital status, and financial position. Inasmuch as I was only twenty-three, I thought my age might disqualify me. And I wasn't married—that also might eliminate me. My education included a three-year college diploma in agriculture. But when I filled out the questionnaire I wrote as if I were a doctor of agronomy, a bachelor of veterinary science, a master of economics, and a budding genius in animal genetics. I put in everything I could think of that would make me eligible for a piece of that Esperance government ground. The most difficult question to answer was the one pertaining to my financial status. I really didn't have any assets. To obscure this deficiency I vastly overvalued such things as my decrepit car, four ponies and their saddlery, and a portable radio. I dreamed up a few other things, fearfully included the few pounds I had in the bank and posted the application with a prayer. In retrospect, I think my principal asset was my dedicated determination to go to Esperance.

The land was being offered at 4 shillings an acre (about 40c) to those who could qualify and I had set my heart on having three thousand acres (the maximum allowed) at a total cost of £400 ($800.00). I was going to become a plutocrat overnight. Of course, in my naïveté I didn't realize that the cost of the land was only a drop in the bucket, and I had no idea that it would cost about 200 shillings ($20) an acre to make it productive. Furthermore, I didn't realize that it was necessary to have several hundred acres producing before it was possible to be self-sustaining. I had a lot to learn.

While I was waiting for a decision on my application, I began planning how to get myself, bag and baggage, to Esperance. I decided that if my application were approved I would go to Esperance and take a job for maybe a year to gain experience in the area before actually working "my land." In other words I would "go native." I thought a job with the local government agricultural research station would be a good idea. I could learn not only what to do and how to do it, but what not to do. And I figured that if a government job wasn't available I could work for one of the pioneering farmers already established at Esperance. Mean-

while, I could develop my land in my spare time—by moonlight, if necessary.

While I was getting ready for my great westward trek, I read with intense interest all the news stories about the Chase syndicate's glowing plans for land development at Esperance. Indeed, Allen Chase was pictured as a great, rich man of international thinking and acclaim who, with his big ideas and agricultural wizardry, boundless money and administrative skills, was going to change the Esperance Plains into a Garden of Eden. He had, the newspapers said, already proved the soundness of his big thinking in developing the gigantic rice farms at Humpty Doo. They gave the impression that Mr. Chase had found solutions to problems which had frustrated Australian farmers for years—how, for example, to control a billion gallons of flood water on flat land a few feet above sea level and how to keep rice plants alive without water during the nine-month dry period. These reports reminded me of the story of the Dutch boy who held the sea back with his thumb in a leaking dyke.

Some of the people I talked to about Esperance reacted with typical Australian skepticism; they took the new stories with a whopping grain of salt. But I took every word as absolute gospel. I still have a news clipping that condenses the optimism of that time:

"Big things are predicted for the southeast of Western Australia following the Chase deal. It is almost certain that Esperance will have its own superphosphate works and abattoirs within ten years. American hotel interests are examining the possibility of 'moving in' on the sleepy town and converting it to a seaside resort which will attract overseas tourists.

"Two new towns are expected to spring up on the coast when hundreds of new farms spread east and west from the present limits.

"However there are those who recall C. J. DeGaris, a man of vision whose dreams of establishing a farming settlement around Kendenup, also in Western Australia, finally were dissipated in an oven. DeGaris planned to divide the land into many farms. With all the produce being purchased by a company, a self-contained, share-the-wealth community

would flourish. Lack of suitable markets and finance led to the downfall of the venture and to the suicide of the man who inspired it.

"But Chase, unlike DeGaris, has his feet firmly on the ground. He is a product of the American school of high finance—shrewd, tough, and courageous. Markets, incidentally, are the least of his worries. He works on the principle, 'If we can grow it, we'll sell it.'"

All this sounded wonderful to me. By now I had convinced myself that this Mr. Chase had founded the great Chase Manhattan Bank, of which I had heard. I was to learn later that he had no connection with that rich institution, and I learned also that it's not very smart to believe all we read in newspapers, hear on a radio, or absorb through myth and legend. But at the time, I reasoned that if Mr. Chase and his American millionaire associates were going to invest in Esperance, the land must really have great potential. And I became even more eager to have a go and get a block of it.

In October or November 1956, word came from the Western Australia Lands and Surveys Department that my application had been approved. I was, as you can imagine, absolutely ecstatic. Shortly after Christmas I drove to Esperance, along with some other successful applicants from our area, to make an exploratory tour. We drove the two thousand miles in a little over ten days, which means we kept rolling night and day.

Esperance was booming and enthusiasm was epidemic. The dusty streets were thronged with farmers, adventurers, speculators, opportunists, and ticket-of-leave men. People slept in cars, tents, and even chairs. Food was scarce and prices high. I got a glimpse of Mr. Chase and was almost transfixed, as if I had been looking at the Second Coming. I had many offers to buy my contract with the Lands and Surveys Department. I could have had a handsome profit without turning a furrow. But I figured that if my plot was worth twice what I was to pay the state for it to someone else, it would be worth it to me.

Like many others, though, I was disappointed when I saw the land I had been allocated. Its stunted scrub growth was tough and I knew it would be hard to clear. The rainfall was reported to be adequate, but there seemed to be little other water available. However, when I visited some of the established farms in the area, I became reinspired. Their pastures were good, subsoil domestic water was plentiful, and I knew that if others could bring the land up to quality, I could too.

Returning home, I began preparations for the major move to Esperance. I walked tall because I felt like a landlord. I had a worthwhile purpose in life, a goal—something important to work for. My father gave me a six-year-old tractor and a fourteen-year-old ex-army truck, which after a considerable amount of work, was ready for the road. I was more than grateful for these two vehicles because they added tremendously to my tangible assets. We loaded the tractor onto the truck and included a thirty-year-old plow which unhappily promptly fell apart when put to the test of pioneering. Among many other things, we also carried a refrigerator and a few pieces of furniture. Finally, we were ready to shove off.

My traveling companion was Bob Summers, a college friend who wanted to go to Esperance in the hope of getting some land for his own. You should have seen us as we started out: that badly overloaded ancient vehicle of war with buckets hanging from it and boxes roped to its sides, and Bob and me grinning confidently from ear to ear.

The first four hundred miles of the two thousand to Esperance were paved—after a fashion. The other sixteen hundred through the dry and isolated areas of the continent were gravel or dirt.

Let me interrupt John Hagon's narrative to point out that the outback roads in Australia for the most part are roads in name only. The distances are so great, the population so scattered, and the money to build roads so scarce that vast stretches are crossed only over rutty tracks. Culverts, drains, and bridges are unheard-of and the runoff of rain storms slashes deep ruts and ditches which make the going not only slow but dangerous. These ruts are filled with bull dust into which a car's wheel can drop up to the frame. Because the roads are so bad and so few, stockmen, until very recent years, instead of trucking

John Hagon sets out for Esperance.

their cattle to market, drove them as far as two thousand miles.

Today the federal government and the State of Western Australia are participating in a crash program to build "beef roads" for the movement by highway of cattle trains to shipping points and killing stations along the coast. Seven million dollars has been allocated for this undertaking, which involves the upgrading and maintaining of hundreds of miles of road through rugged terrain. These will serve to double beef production in areas far removed from killing plants and shipping points, and enable the truck trains to enter regions heretofore inaccessible to them. Volumes of livestock can be delivered to killing centers in the course of a single day as compared to a month or more of droving. These modern beef roads and truck trains also make it possible to release cattle for market at the desirable age of three years instead of six or seven. In the past, such immature animals could not have withstood the rigors of the long overland drives, which only the toughest animals survived.

But John Hagon's drive to Esperance in November 1956 was an horrendous journey across the windswept, sand-blasted, chuck-holed Nullarbor Plain. Back to his story.

Our first day we had only one breakdown. This occurred near the town of West Wyalong in New South Wales and held us up only a few hours. But on the second day, not far from a small town named Goolgowi on the Western Plains, the fan flew off and went through the truck's radiator. Unhappily, there was no welding equipment in Goolgowi, so I had to hitchhike, carrying the radiator, more than a hundred miles to have the cooler repaired. I got back around midnight and found my dejected friend Robert asleep under the truck, sheltered from the faint light of the twinkling stars. As soon as dawn broke, we bolted the radiator back into position and continued our journey. The truck's absolute maximum speed was twenty miles an hour, and we calculated it not by the old broken speedometer but by the mile pegs we passed. Mile after mile on that desolate and monotonous dirt road we would calculate by our watches and the posts the speed of that tired old truck. There were two good reasons for our slow speed; one was the small tires I had bought for the truck because they were cheaper than the recommended standard size; and the other was the tremendous overload we were carrying. We certainly weren't bothered by traffic on those New South Wales plains. All day long we would pass only six to twelve vehicles. Our principal entertainment was counting the kangaroos. If we had been traveling at a normal speed the kangaroos could have posed an accident hazard, but twenty miles an hour is about half the speed a kangaroo can travel.

By the end of the fourth day we had covered some three hundred miles and we felt as tired as the old truck acted. Still we pressed on from dawn until after dark, our toes squinched in apprehension of a breakdown. It came soon enough—a generator fault. The cooling fan was mounted on one end of the generator and without a serviceable generator the fan couldn't operate; it vibrated so much that the studs which clamped it to the generator came loose. Each town we came to we tried to buy the necessary parts to repair the generator. One garage man we talked to said, "Why, that bloody old truck is fourteen years old. Chances are you'll not find a part for it in all of Australia." He asked us where we were bound and when we told him he said, "Good grief! —that's all the way across the desert," meaning the Nullarbor Plain. "You'll never in God's name make it. She'll boil her head off."

We had no recourse; we had to run without a fan. I drove until the engine got dangerously hot. Then we stopped and waited until it cooled off. It was start and stop and wait. After two days of this slow torture, we reached a big town called Mildura on the Victorian border, and it was there that our prayers were answered and I found the part we so desperately needed.

By the end of the first week we had covered seven hundred miles and had reached Port Augusta. We were close to exhaustion. We had slept fitfully, we were undernourished, unshaven, and unbathed. We must have looked a sorry lot. We decided to stop for the night in Port Augusta, pay for a hotel room, enjoy the luxury of a bath, eat a good hot meal, and get some sleep. As we drove up and stopped before the hotel we had selected, some army servicemen walked past and one of them said to his companion, "Have a look, mates —everything but the kitchen sink." Whereupon my friend Bob jumped down in front of them and yelled, "It's on the back, Jack. Have a bloody look!" One look at Bob's bearded, angry face and the servicemen did not tarry to argue.

I don't think I'll ever forget that shower we had at Port Augusta. It was sheer ecstasy. Unable to sleep that night, despite, or maybe on account of, the soft bed and pillow, I thought of what the garage man had said about the truck's inability to make it across the Nullarbor Plain. Things always look black to me in the middle of the night, and I decided that in the morning I would investigate the possibility of freighting the truck and ourselves by railroad to Esperance. The next day I went to the office of the Trans-continental Railway and was advised that the cost would be approximately £250 ($500)!

That kind of an expenditure was definitely out of the question. All I had left of the £300 my parents had given me to help establish myself on my new farm was £280 and it was unthinkable that I should sacrifice my whole nest egg just to get to my destination. So we cranked up the old bus and drove on.

The only times we stopped for the next four days were to buy fuel and to repair the fuel and oil lines. The lines kept breaking because the road was like a corrugated washboard. Bob watched the oil gauge like a hawk and as soon as it dropped to zero we would switch off the engine, rattle to a halt, repair the fracture, and then start out again.

When we were 450 miles from our destination, and within 20 miles of a service station–motel, we found we had broken all of the truck's springs except the main one on the rear left-hand side. By this time we were immune to misfortune and a certain dogged, patient philosophy had evolved in us. If the engine had dropped out I would simply have hoisted it onto my back and, operating purely on reflex, trudged with it to the next service station.

By repacking the load as best we could so that my precious possessions wouldn't shake off, we crept on, the truck and

John Hagon (at the gate to his “palace”): *“Fair Dinkum, mate, does it LOOK like the Rockefeller Estate?!. . . .”*

the load jolting as if the wheels were square. Eventually, we made it to the motel where the owner, a friend-in-need if ever there was one, loaned me his acetylene set and took me to his scrap heap of broken cars. I took some springs from one of the dead vehicles and fitted them to my truck. After a day and a half of work, we were on the road again.

We covered the next 450 miles to Esperance in three days, driving almost nonstop. The total trip took sixteen days, which means we averaged about 120 miles a day. We arrived at our destination in jubilant spirits—at the ungodly hour of four in the morning. For want of a better place, we camped in the Esperance railway yard.

The next day we drove the thirty-two miles of sandy road to my beloved three thousand virgin acres and pitched the tent we had borrowed. I was on my own land—heaven on earth.

John Hagon was only one among hundreds who came to Esperance during that time, bringing with them lots of hope and very little money. But John had something more precious than money to invest. He had youth, energy, earnestness, integrity, and a receptive, schooled, and disciplined mind. His tense, miserable experience getting to "the land of promise" was duplicated by many others, who came as the Argonauts had come to California in the 1850's and as the Oakies had come in the economically depressed 1930's. Like the Oakies, the Aussie migrants were strong and determined and they have survived.

CHAPTER TEN

Field Marshal John Hagon Takes Over

The winter season 1956–57 was very poor in rainfall—the lowest in fifty-seven years. In the area we were working rainfall totaled something over nine inches; eighteen to twenty-four inches is normal. But I don't think our first year's failure at Esperance can be charged to the lack of water. More rainfall might have helped, but the core of our failure was bound up in our hit-or-miss methods in trying to establish a stand of pasture in one year.

One newspaper headlined a report on our Esperance operation: AMERICAN KNOW-HOW DIDN'T WORK.

We investors had lost the cost of the clover and grass seed, the cost of the minerals and superphosphates, and the cost of the plowing and planting. We had also lost much of our enthusiasm and hope for Esperance. But some of the plowing had been effective where the ground was lying fallow, as required for successful planting. Furthermore, some of the superphosphates and minerals were in the ground. So our effort had not been a total loss.

Nevertheless, most of the United States investors picked up their dollars and withdrew from the scene. And in truth, I was getting more than a little tired of pouring even discounted dollars down a rathole.

On the other hand, I had visited a few farms which had been developed in the area by Australian farmers and they were "giving it a good go." The ghost of Horatio Alger, Jr., was sitting on my shoulder again, and I was convinced that if someone else could grow good pasture in that sandy soil, I could, too. Besides, I can't stand negatives, especially failure. Another reason I just couldn't fold my tent and slink away was that by now Australia was in my blood: I *liked* it, and particularly I liked Esperance.

So I decided I would try once more to develop the ten thousand acres I had bought. Once I had made this decision, the next order of business was to find a really competent manager. I was in Esperance so little of the time, I had to have not only someone to supervise the farm operation, but a man with a long view who could make decisions, plan ahead, and hire and fire effectively.

It so happened that John Hagon's three thousand acres are just a few miles up the road from my block. From time to time when he needed work and we needed help, he would do odd jobs for us. John had long since used up his nest egg and like so many before him, he had found out that knowledge and a strong back are of little use without money to buy the necessary minerals for the hungry land. He had learned this was no place to poor-boy a farm. Superphosphates cost $30 a ton and it required 150 pounds of the stuff for *each* acre *every* year to produce a pasture. So John had cleared what he could of his land and in between times looked for work to support himself and, hopefully, to save enough for his fertilizer requirements.

The first time I met John I was driving past his place with Allen Chase and some others to see how the work was going on my land. We stopped to have a look at what John, as a native Australian, was doing. I asked him why a young man like himself would want to come away out here to this godforsaken place to settle, and I remember he was very definite and succinct in his reply.

"I came to Esperance because the land is cheap and the rain-

fall is reliable," he said, "and because an opportunity exists for a young man with limited capital."

Allen asked him why he was seeding only a hundred acres. "Because that's all the money I have to buy seed and superphosphate," John replied.

I remember as we were leaving, Allen said, "That young man is going to be a big success." As things are turning out, Allen was right.

The Esperance Plains contractor continued plowing, much of it ineffectually, through the spring and summer. The tractors, each drawing its four wide-spread plows, traveled in a straight line for eighteen miles before turning back. The first time they went out and came to the end of the eighteen miles, their supervisor stopped them, saying, "We'll make camp here. Otherwise the bugger will have us in Adelaide." And so it may have seemed to those weary drivers, although Adelaide is some thirteen hundred miles from Esperance.

Eighteen square miles of the area that the company plowed was mine. It came to be known as Linkletter's Place, and its headquarters was some sixty miles from Esperance over a corrugated, dusty, country road.

John Hagon first came to work for me on my own place as a temporary helper in 1958. But the day he signed on, my wheel of fortune in Australia began to reverse itself and the production graph of Esperance began to rise. It has been ten years since John Hagon became my manager, and he has developed one of the most fertile, productive, and efficient farms in all of Australia.

John was like a powerful aspirin to a migraine headache. The aches and pains didn't disappear all at once, but little by little nagging worries and frustrating perplexities disappeared. And suddenly one day I realized we were having fun. The planning was constructive, the growth steady, and the future bright.

John is more than a farmer—he is a farm manager. Heads of great corporations spend most of their time and much of their money seeking men with his abilities. If I had been making airplane parts, building bridges, or franchising a chain of beauty shops with John in charge, he would have done the same thorough, solid job of planning and performance. He knows how to organize every farming operation and can do each of them superbly himself. He is a good judge of men and has the self-discipline that makes him a good teacher. He is loyal not only to his employer but to his men as well. He is familiar with bookkeeping and knows to the penny how much each ranch operation should cost. From the household budget for his family to the mileage of a tractor, John keeps a sharp eye on costs. He has schedules, quotas, performance graphs, and summaries.

The housekeeping on Linkletter's Place is immaculate. Every tool has its place and each piece is checked in and checked out as if it were made of gold. It seems as if John knows every sheep by name. He knows how much wool each should produce and he knows when each ewe should lamb. But the rams are his special pride and joy. Any ram on Linkletter's Place that is not properly exhausted at the end of the breeding season is shipped pronto to the meatworks. He expects them to earn their keep.

In short, John Hagon brought order out of chaos and ran my place with the authority of a field marshal. He insisted that we buy ewes and rams of top quality and breed only the best of them so that the wool marked *Linkletter's Place* would command premium prices at the auctions. It was his suggestion that we raise cattle as well as sheep, because the diversification would give us flexibility in case of a drastic change in world markets. He resisted the temptation to plant quick cash crops that had not been proven and contented himself with raising wheat and barley, reliable crops which are conservatively profitable.

And he kept urging me to get the "amenities" for the people who live and work on the place. "Amenities" is a word that has almost been forgotten in the United States. It is a pioneer word with rural roots and full of meaning for people who live where there are no paved roads, telephones, electric lights, schools, stores, or inside plumbing. It roughly means the civilities—all those convenient things which people who live in cities take for granted, like running water out of a tap, a refrigerator, instant light. It means a place to shop and it means prompt mail delivery. It means a hot bath, a bus to take the children to school, and it means the school itself. It means a good stove and a screen to keep out the "bities," which is what the Australian kids call mosquitoes.

When we started Linkletter's Place, there were no amenities and lots of bities. We were sixty miles from Esperance to the west and ninety miles from Baladonia to the north. We had to start from scratch, as pioneering homesteaders started in America a century ago. First shelter, then pasture to feed the livestock, and finally fences to control the livestock.

We needed roads we could roll on, and this meant bridges, culverts, bulldozing, grading. We needed lumber and nails and cement and gasoline and oil and medicine and anything else you care to mention. And most of all we needed people with skills and the will to work. When I think of the obstacles we had to overcome and the backbreaking work it took to overcome them, I marvel that we had the audacity to start.

At Linkletter's we added the amenities as fast as we could. We had neat little two-bedroom houses built with good kitchens, inside toilets, and running water. We graded good roads to crisscross the ten thousand acres, and planted trees all along their many miles to lend shade, break the monotony of the flatland, and screen the wind. Planted ten years ago as saplings, these trees have now grown to heights of fifteen to twenty feet, and in the hot weather the sheep and cattle love to lie down in their shade.

When John Hagon first came to work for me as a farm hand, he was paid $200 a month. Within a year he was earning $4,000 a year and this was increased to $4,500, in addition to which he received bonus payments each year of about $2,000. By 1960 he was doing so well financially that he decided he could afford a family. Life in the outback without a woman is "like a ship without a sail, like a boat without a rudder, like a fish without a tail." When John had time for social life, he dated a Perth-trained nurse named Jennifer Osbourne. She was a lovely brunette with a quick smile and a happy disposition, and in March 1960, John took a few days off from his managerial duties at our place to marry her. Jenny had grown up in the country and was a perfect choice to live so far from town on a developing property.

John brought Jenny "home" to Linkletter's Place. The house they occupied grew from a storage shed which had been built by the Esperance Plains Company in 1957. Subsequently it had been converted into bachelor living quarters, and just before leaving for Perth to get married, John thoughtfully added a laundry and a clothesline for his bride. Obviously, he expected Jenny to get right to work, and I have no doubt she did. Later, to make the shed look more like a house, he had a carpenter cover it with siding. After a few more alterations supervised by Jenny, the house became as it is today, a some-

Entrance to Linkletter's Place.

what jerry-built and haphazard affair but homey and comfortable.

As I write this, plans are being prepared to build a new homestead on the property. It will be considerably more modern and in keeping with the present size and value of the ranch. In addition to being a home for the Hagons, there will be space for guests as well, and when Lois and I go there each spring, we will have a pleasant place to stay.

John writes characteristically about his new house: *It is not our aim to have the biggest or the most expensive house in the region (one is being built now that is half again as big and on property owned by an Australian syndicate which has recently taken up land at Esperance), but to have a dwelling built to our requirements now and for the future.*

The Hagons now have three children: Angela Jane, born in May 1961; Philippa Joan, born in October 1963; and Richard John, born in August 1965.

The Hagons have done well. John is now paid between

$10,000 and $12,000 a year, plus $500 for extraordinary expenses for managing Linkletter's Place. I use the indefinite word "between" because his salary fluctuates somewhat, being based on a fixed sum plus a percentage of sales. In a year or two he should be making $15,000 annually for his services on our place and an additional sum, based on a percentage of sales, for managing the Condingup property.

Allen Chase's original prediction is certainly coming true. John Hagon has earned a national reputation in Australia; he owns a fine small property of his own, and his annual income from the Linkletter property puts him in the bracket of top earners down under.

CHAPTER ELEVEN

Outback Amenities and Jackeroos

In the beginning, children on the station got their schooling by radio, through the unique school of the air. Because of the great distances between towns and sheep-and-cattle stations and mines of the outback, Australia has a network of radio stations which were set up by her famous "flying doctor" service. Every settlement has a two-way radio and the emergency-call circuit is manned around the clock. Night or day, a call for help gets action, either over the air or in person!

The same radio network is used to teach the outback children. The school of the air borrows the doctor's network for four hours a day, during the week, to educate youngsters who otherwise would have no elementary schooling at all. At Esperance, for example, the radio was used to broadcast lessons to the children within a four-hundred-mile area. At 9:45 every weekday morning children who have no other access to school gather around the radio loudspeaker to hear their teacher open the day's session with a song. He may ask Elizabeth, 250 miles away, to repeat the song, which she does, and so do all the others in the "class." Tommy, 130 miles east, says she sang it too high. There ensues a laughing argument back and forth over the air as the "class" uses microphones and transmitters to join in the discussion. Each youngster sits at a table with a microphone and listens to the teacher. When a specific child is queried by name, he or she will press a switch, answer the question, and the radio carries the answer back to all students and the teacher.

The teacher conducts the school of the air with one hand on a switch and the other on a volume control knob. She will ask a pupil at one station to recite "The calf went down the path to take a bath in the afternoon," as part of a speech lesson. And when the pupil has repeated the lines, the teacher will ask that the word "the" before afternoon be emphasized. The pupil will repeat, enunciating properly. Meanwhile all the other pupils throughout the school area will hear the recitation as they would if they were all in the same classroom.

"I think I'll ask Hubert to spell water," says the teacher. And from a far-off place that is athirst for it comes the childish voice: "w-a-t-e-r, water."

The classes in the school of the air extend from the first through the eighth grades. Books carrying the lessons come by mail, and every day the children answer a roll call.

Itinerant teachers visit isolated homesteads at least twice a year, traveling in vans with projectors, film, tape recorders, books, samples of work charts, and other aids to lend the children personal assistance and encouragement and to give advice to their parents. Many outback cattle-and-sheep stations also engage tutors to live on the stations and instruct the children.

When pupils have graduated and are ready for high school, the more prosperous settlers send their children to boarding school in the larger towns.

There are two systems of education in Australia—state and private. About four-fifths of the children of school age attend state schools and one-fifth attend private schools. Primary schooling starts in January of the year in which a child is five years old. After seven years of primary schooling the child transfers automatically to a secondary school. The secondary education consists of five years, divided into two parts: the first three years are basic and nearly all students complete them; the next two years are required for admittance to a university.

Through the radio hookup, people who live in isolated areas not only can call for a doctor or get an early education for their children, but also can send messages to town. And when the radio is not being used for teaching and there is a lull between an emergency or business call, the ladies of the outback use the system as a party-line telephone. Mrs. Borden of Dumbellyungger will ask Lizzie Jensen to respond from Kanellyupjen. And when Lizzie's voice comes over the air, Mrs. Borden may ask for a recipe or inquire about a sick child. Or a lady from Condingup may come on the air and ask anxiously if anyone listening should see her husband go by in a rickety Toyota, would they please stop him and tell him to come right home.

Quite often, listening to the wireless is better entertainment than one could get on commercial radio. It is full of drama and sometimes melodrama.

The flying doctor radio service was inaugurated by the Reverend John Flynn, a Presbyterian minister, in 1928, and his contribution to the nation has been commemorated by a memorial and shrine at Alice Springs, which is almost at the exact center of the continent. His world-famous service has brought medical help to tremendously vast areas where there are no hospitals and no doctors.

Nowhere else in the world is radio such an essential part of everyday life as it is in central and western Australia. There are twelve medical posts, each with a resident doctor and pilot. Each station averages two thousand medical calls a year and handles about thirty-four telegram messages. When a doctor gets a call for medical help, he does not necessarily get into an airplane and fly to the patient, although he is quick to do this if there is an emergency. First, though, he tries to determine the seriousness of the ailment and if there is no danger of death or complications, he prescribes treatment by radio. Every outback ranch or mission has a two-way radio and a standard medical kit with numbered drawers and labeled containers located near the microphone.

A conversation with the flying doctor might go like this: "This is Linkletter's Place, Esperance. We have a jackeroo

The school house at Linkletter's Place.

with a high temperature. His pulse is slow and his tongue is coated brown."

"Right, mate. He doesn't sound as though he's going to croak. Try a level teaspoon of that yellow stuff in drawer number two, marked B. If that doesn't do it, and his eyes look dull, open drawer number five and give him a shot of the pills marked liver. Got it?"

"Roger. Good on you, Doc. Over and out."

If other drugs are indicated, these will be dispatched to the patient by air. And if the ailment is serious, the doctor will hop in a plane and hightail it to the patient.

As an extra added attraction to our employees, we decided to build a school. The state, I was informed, would supply a teacher if we could recruit twelve children. So John went to our neighbors who lived within twenty-five miles of our headquarters and enlisted their help. We finally got enough children enrolled to warrant state help and built a neat little one-room schoolhouse. Living quarters were provided on the grounds for the teacher.

Because the nearest store was in Esperance, two hours away by a bumpy dirt road, I helped finance an ambitious young man to start a general store in the area that had been reserved for a townsite. We even built tennis courts and a playground. While we were laying the tennis courts, John asked me facetiously when we were going to build a movie theater. It wasn't long before John himself was running educational movies for our young future farmers.

We kept adding employees as we needed and could get them. The two big and continuing problems that plague underdeveloped Australia are money and manpower. At our place, I provided the money, but the manpower problem was John's responsibility. He looked for families because, isolated as the station is, only those men who brought wives could be expected to stay for any length of time.

There were plenty of drifters we could hire; semiskilled farm workers who float from place to place and never seem to put down roots. And there are always a few "good blokes" who are content to do a fair job, but lack that extra something we moderns call motivation, otherwise known as "get-up-and-go." In order to get people to do the outstanding work he wanted done on our station, John advertised for jackeroos, the Aussie word for apprentice farmers. Most often, jackeroos are young men out for adventure or to have a go at work they are not sure they want to do. Then again, they may be boys who have to work because they don't have the money to go to college.

John took out advertisements in country newspapers describing the kind of man he was looking for, the work he wanted him to do, and the prospects for promotion. He pictured Linkletter's Place as a sort of farm-school which would give practical lessons that could prepare a young man to become a farmer-manager. The advertisements brought quick results. We had our pick of a number of ambitious young men, many of them from smaller stations who wanted to learn the facts about sheep-raising and how to handle modern equipment.

We hired six of them. They signed a two-year contract and

were provided good quarters and a cook of their own. John acquired a movie projector, films from the Agriculture Department, and, using our schoolhouse at night, taught these young men things about farming that he couldn't teach them in the field. That was his movie theater!

John introduced the jackeroo system in the hope that he could train young men not only to raise the standard of work on our place but to benefit agriculture generally. And that is the way it has worked out. These young men are turning out a quality of work never before seen in Esperance or, I venture, anywhere in Australia. John has filled them with pride and enthusiasm for their work and with devotion to their jobs. Their morale is so high that they are an inspiration to the older hands on the place.

Under this program, we hire four jackeroos a year. Of the eight "graduated" so far, four have become successful farmers and one has proved to be outstanding.

Wages are based on age. An eighteen-year-old, for example, will be started at $14.70 a week, plus his keep. After one year he is raised to $18.35, plus his keep. For these wages he works and/or goes to school about forty-four to fifty hours a week. All jackeroos get three weeks' vacation with pay each year. If this sounds like a lot of work for small pay, remember this is Australia in the outback, not Hollywood!

The jacks work on an award system, which is to say, they earn points for every skill they master during the two-year training period. They get direct instruction in all phases of farm management as well as free correspondence courses in agriculture and farm management. They must score well in both their schooling and their practical training. They attend field demonstrations and farm tours conducted in the area, and in the classroom John provides counsel augmented by chalk talks and pertinent films. Lectures and demonstrations are also given by visiting authorities from the Agriculture Department and commercial firms. For example, a wool expert from a brokerage house may be in the area, and John will ask him to talk to the jackeroos about wool-marketing; a representative from a drug firm will lecture on internal parasites which afflict sheep and cattle; the veterinary surgeon from the Agriculture Department will do a postmortem on a sheep. The department also supplies lecturers with special knowledge of cereal-growing, animal husbandry, lamb-marketing, mulesing, stock inspection, as well as tractor-driving, machinery maintenance, welding, water conservation, windmill maintenance, gardening, milking, and any number of other aspects of farming. The jacks also get instruction in budgeting, bookkeeping, and management procedures.

In effect, what John Hagon conducts at Linkletter's Place for the jackeroos is a two-year agricultural college.

I think it should be noted that, although we are deep in the sheep industry, at Esperance we do not have sheepherders *per se* as they do in other countries—the United States, the Pyrenees, the Middle East, and other parts of the world. All sheep at Esperance are closely controlled in fenced paddocks of about two hundred acres each. The only time a herder is needed is when the sheep have eaten the grass in one paddock and a gate must be opened into the next. Close control and rotational pasturing eliminates the sheepherder as we know him—that lonely figure who, with his dog, follows the sheep in their eternal quest for grass. Jackeroos and unit managers at Esperance tend the sheep between other chores, and they live not in tents but in comfortable homes.

The jacks are busiest at lambing time, when they are on duty for twenty-four hours a day to assist the lambing ewes. In between, they build or mend fences, maintain the windmills and watering troughs, look out for and treat any injured sheep, and keep their station and its equipment in repair.

As of this writing, we have five families living on our place. Together with the jackeroos, the working staff totals eleven. Our census grows, of course, if we add the wives and children.

Twelve structures providing housing, storage, and areas for specific farm tasks, plus a plant for generating electricity make up the headquarters of our station. Equipment includes three tractors, four utility trucks, two motorcycles, and three trailers for hauling sheep and cattle. There are twenty-seven windmills and fifty-four water troughs. One hundred miles of fence surround and partition the place.

The paddock fencing, which John Hagon developed, is unique. Fence posts are spaced ninety-nine feet apart. Between the posts nine strands of smooth wire, almost as heavy as telephone wire, have been stretched tautly. Barbed wire is bad for sheep or cattle. When dogs drive a herd into a paddock, the sheep tend to crowd against the fence and many would get cut by barbed wire. So John adapted the American idea of stretching strands of smooth wire under tension, drawing it taut as one might tune a guitar. For fence posts he avoided the tea wood, which is generally used throughout the area, and chose *pinus radiata*, which is durable and termite-resistant.

There are a great many paddocks on the place, so necessarily there are a lot of gates. When we are driving around in a jeep or truck, it is a nuisance to have to stop to open and close all these gates. John has designed and is experimenting with a piece of equipment that may solve the problem. The device looks like a pair of skis fastened to the front frame of a jeep. The skis project beyond the front bumper and when the jeep comes up to a fence, the ski pushes the elastic wire down flat on the ground so the vehicle can pass over. Once the weight of the jeep clears, the tension-sprung wires would spring back into position. If this idea works, it not only will save time and frustration, but could reduce the number of gates that we would have to build.

We use two kinds of gates now: the standard swinging type, which are necessary so we can move the sheep from one paddock to another; and the cattle-guard type—a series of rails which project from the ground in an unfenced area—which sheep and cattle, fearing they will become entangled, will not cross. In addition, John is presently trying a new kind of "psychological" cattle guard which has been used on main highways in cattle and sheep areas of the American West. For open spread rails across the road, the psycho guard substitutes painted black and white stripes extending across the highway.

Aborigines appraise the new telephone lines: *"So they've built a kangaroo-proof fence—so where's the bottom plurry wire?"*

"The line's engaged!!" New settlers found many uses for the telegraph poles and the wire.

The cattle and horses mistake these stripes for actual barriers and refuse to cross the painted lines.

John Hagon is always trying to work out new methods of doing things. He's always alert to ways of saving time and money. Recently, he wrote: *The machine we are using to windrow the hay was an adaptation or modification of an existing rotary slasher manufactured in Melbourne. I converted our existing model to do the same job as the manufacturer's latest model. The modification took me approximately five hours and saved us between four and five hundred dollars.* He is using a root gouging machine developed by a small Western Australia manufacturer and it has revolutionized the clearing of land. Only a few years ago roots had to be dug out by hand.

These are just a few of the innovations John Hagon has made at our place. He has worked hard to shape the station into a beautiful, prosperous enterprise, and the progress he has made is nothing less than phenomenal. His predictions work out with uncanny accuracy. Every year we expect to clear another thousand to fifteen hundred acres for future planting, and every year we will plow and plant the acreage which was cleared the year before. Thus every year more land is cultivated and every year more sheep are added to our flock.

Meanwhile, I have never missed an opportunity to urge the Premier of Western Australia in Perth, my friend the Honorable David Brand, to help all of the folks out our way with projects that can reasonably be done only by the government—more bitumen roads and telephone service, for example. Slowly the paved roads have crept out from Esperance to our station and beyond. We are no longer at the end of the line. When we Americans came to Esperance, there were about thirty established farmers; now there are seven hundred, and the flying doctor service and the shortwave radios have been replaced by the telephone.

Progress—it's beautiful!

CHAPTER TWELVE

I Have an Estrogen Headache!

Despite the great job John Hagon has done and the progress that has been made, there have been surprising setbacks and bitter disappointments at Esperance.

One of the most costly problems was also a frustrating mystery. For some reason, many of our ewes would abort their lambs and either die in the process or become permanently sterile. We had to solve the problem in a hurry because each year Linkletter's Place lost thousands of mother sheep and their lambs. At first we thought it might be a disease caused by the bite of an insect, but thorough research ruled that out. We wondered if the abortions might be hereditary, but this possibility was easily eliminated. We finally decided that the problem had to be in something the sheep were eating. The big question was What?

The last thing to be suspected was the gorgeous green subterranean clover which grew so luxuriantly and which the sheep consumed in large quantities. The clover was examined and we discovered that it contained estrogen, a female hormone which disturbs the reproductive process. This substance was the deadly enemy. It literally turned the ewe's uterus inside out. And since the clover had been planted throughout our pasture, it took years to eradicate it and substitute a new, safe

Pioneer and a Merino take stock of each other.

strain of clover. As "pioneers" this was a part of the price we paid to open up this fertile new country and make it easier for those who followed.

Then there were dingoes. These incredibly ingenious wild dogs preyed on our flocks, dragged the young lambs under the wire fences, and slashed their throats.

The dingo is both a menace and a mystery—a menace because of his destructiveness as a killer of lambs and young calves, and a mystery because no one is sure of his origin. He may be the world's oldest type of dog. There is the intriguing probability that the dingo came to Australia with the aborigines as a domesticated animal twenty thousand years ago. He is part of aborigine myth and legend and the aborigine is best able to domesticate him.

Wild dingoes will not accept an injured or deformed dog as a member of their groups. Knowing this, the aborigine woman will break a foreleg of the puppy as soon as she captures him. Though crippled, the dingo can still hunt after the leg has

Aborigine woman and her dingo hunting companion.

healed, and he becomes a constant, utterly dedicated hunting companion of the aborigine woman. The dingo hunts, travels, and sleeps with his mistress and dies with her when she is no longer able to fend for herself.

Wild dingoes are a most curious admixture of cunning, savagery, and playfulness. Unlike wolves, they do not travel in packs. At evening when the air is still, the wild dingo, his belly empty, will come out of hiding. Depending almost entirely on scent, he will inch up to a flock of sheep, single out a victim, and with one spring have it by a leg. Dingoes never bark, but after they have eaten, and especially in the early hours of the morning, they will raise their noses and howl mournfully at the heavens like coyotes. Whenever we heard that sound at night, and it came to us all too frequently, we could chalk off another lamb. Dingoes will often kill a dozen or more sheep just for the hell of it.

To get rid of the dingoes we took a green bone and treated the marrow with cyanide. We wired these bones to fence posts, and each one would account for four or five dingoes before it was wholly consumed. During the last couple of years the dingo has retreated into the virgin outback and is no longer much of a problem in the fast-growing area around Esperance.

To me, the most horrifying of all the enemies of sheep are crows. I had never known that birds could maim and kill sheep, but they do, and in the most diabolical way. Swooping down from the sky, these scavengers will attack the young lambs, picking at their eyes and anuses. The mother ewe will frantically run back and forth trying to protect her baby until she actually collapses from exhaustion. Then the crows will descend upon the expired ewe and have a feast.

We partially solved the crow problem by building huge cages in which we placed a dead sheep as a lure for the crows. When the birds flew in to get at the meat, they were trapped. We also declared "open season" on them, as we had on the geese in the rice paddies at Humpty Doo, and hunters killed them by the hundreds.

Rabbits were another problem—they loved to eat the pasture.

We used a poison on them so deadly that one single grain would kill not only a rabbit, but a dog, a sheep, or a cow as well. The formula, which has to be distributed under government control, is 1 percent poison grain to 90 percent good grain. A ten-ton caterpillar tractor would follow the poisoner and cover over the treated rabbit warrens with a scraper blade.

It is intriguing that wherever man finds an Eden he sets out to introduce, as it were, some snakes. And so it was in Australia when homesick transplants from Mother England wanted hares to run against the beagles, foxes for the foxhounds, and cats for the mice and contentment at the fireside.

Rabbits were first introduced into Australia in 1859, and that importation proved to be a near-disastrous mistake. Twenty-four of the multipliers were liberated on an estate near Geelong, Victoria. During the ensuing six years, the estate's owner killed twenty thousand of the creatures, and then appealed to the government for help. In a single year, at the height of the plague, the government of New South Wales spent £1.5 million trying to control the pests. It is estimated that if it weren't for the millions of rabbits (all descendants of those original twenty-four), the pastures of Australia could now support 20 percent more sheep.

Well, we got rid of a lot of the rabbits around our place with myxomatosis, but the trouble now is that the remaining ones seem to have developed an immunity to everything we've tried so far. Australian scientists are trying to find new ways to curb the rabbit population explosion. They have their work cut out for them because one male and one female rabbit, under moderate conditions, can produce nine million descendants in a three-year period. That's quite a production record!

Scientists have been painstakingly prying into the habits of rabbits and these gentlemen have discovered that a rabbit's territorial boundaries are staked out by the dominant male in his or her group. In a process called chinning, the dominant male brushes his chin over twigs and stones bordering the land that he claims. A gland on his chin deposits a distinctive scent that makes his own group feel secure but warns away outsiders.

By simulating these scents the scientists hope to ring pasturelands with odors that will exclude marauding nonresident rabbits. Another hope is that false chin trails may lead the unsuspecting hares directly to poisoned bait. That ought to fix the little blankety-blank multipliers.

Next to the estrogen in the grass, our greatest enemy is a blowfly. This vicious pest finds a haven in the moist wrinkles around and under the tail of the big Merino sheep. There they lay their eggs. This reproductive procedure is called fly-strike, and hardly a Merino escapes. The eggs left by the strike hatch quickly, and if they are not removed, the maggots that hatch from the eggs burrow under the skin and eat the sheep alive. Sprays will arrest the fly pestilence temporarily, but in a few days a new batch of blowflies are back laying eggs again.

Many years ago a surgical procedure called mulesing was developed to prevent the infection of fly-strike, and we are using it extensively on our place. The procedure has been such a boon to Australia that the man who perfected it, J. H. W. Mules, is a candidate for knighthood.

In the surgical operation, a skilled worker clips the outer skin fold of the sheep with huge hand shears, removing the skin from the area around the anus and vagina in a circle twelve inches in diameter. This leaves the animal's backside bare, and since no moisture or excrement can collect, the fly-strike of the blowfly is not attracted. Even the tail loses its wool and skin.

All the Merinos at our place are treated this way, and the first time you see one going away from you the effect is startling. His buttocks look somewhat like the naked baboon. Unfortunately, blowflies may still strike in the other wrinkles of a sheep's body, and we still have to go through the "dip" process to eliminate parasites including ticks and lice.

It is worth noting, I think, that many years ago an Australian sheep rancher got the bright idea that the more skin surface a sheep has the more room there would be for wool to grow. So he bred a sheep, the present Australian Merino, with many deep, loose folds of skin. For this great contribution to the

Mulesing—a necessary precaution.

wool-growing industry in general and to Australia in particular, he was knighted by the Queen of England. And then came the blowflies and mulesing to eliminate the excess folds of skin on the Merino.

Another problem in Australia, though not a particularly severe one, is the emu. This great ostrich-like bird is one of the worst offenders in trampling crops, particularly up and down a fence line. For no apparent reason at all, these zany creatures will go berserk over a fair-sized paddock of ripening grain and in no time at all it is flat as the proverbial pancake.

The emu is Australia's largest bird and is second in size only to the ostrich. Found in most parts of the country, it is a ground nester. The female lays eight or nine large green eggs during the brooding period, each of which weighs about a pound and a half. Emus are unpopular with farmers not only because they trample crops but because they spread weed seed and sometimes mutilate lambs.

You only have to say *emu* to an Australian (the bird ap-

Emu watcher: *"Ssh—Just tiptoe quietly away. If you scare 'em they'll trample the whole bloody forty thousand acres!!"*

pears with the kangaroo on Australia's coat-of-arms) to make him laugh. In all conditions and under any circumstances these birds are the zaniest creatures on earth. Confronted by danger they take off at great speed, going in several directions at once.

One of our neighbors at Esperance chased a flock of emus in his old car in an attempt to scare them off his pasture. He kept shooting at them with his shotgun, but as the race progressed he ran out of ammunition. Rolling along beside them, he began throwing anything he could find loose in the car, including the jack and crank-handle. After a chase of several miles the birds leaped a fence and gave him the brush. In turning his car around, the overheated engine stalled and our frustrated neighbor had to walk back those miles to retrieve the crank-handle before he could restart the car. All the way he imagined he could hear the emus cackling at his ignominious defeat.

While we're on the subject of Australia's odd creatures, we should include some kind words about one of Australia's and the world's most unique what-you-may-call-its. Of all the many extraordinary forms of fauna that this continent supports, none has been of so much interest to naturalists, it seems, as the little fur-bearing animal-bird called the platypus.

When this creature was first discovered, it was called *Paradoxus,* because it really is a paradox. It is neither fish nor fowl nor reptile, but apparently a little of all three—another fantastic example of nature's inexhaustible variety. However, for classification purposes it is considered an animal.

Platypuses (or platypusi, if you prefer) inhabit freshwater streams and pools of northern Australia and Tasmania. They have a soft fur coat that has been so badly tailored it is many sizes too large; indeed, it is like a five-year-old in her mother's full-length mink. If you pick up a platypus by its skin you get the feeling he can turn in his skin and bite you from the other end. The fur is shaded from mahogany on the outer portion to gray next to the skin. This shiny material is so beautiful that it is highly prized in the fur trade, and many a platypus has wound up around the neck of a model.

Motorized emu hunter: *"Fetch 'im, boy!!"*

These little fellows vary in length from fifteen to twenty inches. Their paws are webbed as well as clawed, and the webs on their forepaws are so overextended they walk on their knuckles to keep the sharp claws from piercing the webs of their own feet. Their heads terminate like a duck's in an astonishing broad bill, which is flanked by tiny, beady black eyes. Their internal organs are amazingly contradictory: the platypus has the heart of a mammal, but its reproductory organs are like those of a reptile. It hatches its young from eggs and then suckles them. Before laying her eggs, the female digs a breeding burrow that precisely conforms to her own shape. At the end of her breeding she deposits one round soft-shelled egg resembling that of a snake. At other times she may lay three eggs and fasten them all together in a triangle so that none will be lost from the others.

The male platypus has a poisonous spike on a back leg, and this is his only means of defense. Despite his utterly unlikely and exotic appearance, his diet is restricted to fresh angleworms.

Although platypuses can stay under water only a few minutes, they gather their food from the bottom of rivers and pools. They find the worms by feel because when they dive, they close their eyes, ears, and nostrils.

I saw some platypuses living on a diet of fresh garden worms in the zoo at Sydney. Their cage contained a pool where they could feed in shallow water and there was a tunnel to an underground shelter. I was amused by the legend on their sanctuary: PLATYPUSURY.

CHAPTER THIRTEEN

Marsupials and "Darlings"

During the time that things were beginning to shape up at Linkletter's Place in Esperance, the Chase Syndicate, whose initial planting had failed, had become inactive. Dr. Morton Love, called in again by the company, confirmed that the failure of the first year's crop was the result of poor planting techniques and an unfavorable weather season. The syndicate, he said, had taken a risk in trying to get things done quickly and had lost the gamble. This was not news. It was pretty obvious by that time that the routine operations had been done either too hurriedly or in the wrong season.

In January 1959, the Esperance Plains Company sold nearly 60,000 acres of its undeveloped land and in February of that year it returned 21,000 acres to the state. The money was simply running out.

This action by the Esperance Plains Company, which had started out with such glowing hopes and promises, was an admission of failure, and it was a severe setback to the entire Esperance district. Many people lost confidence in the area.

Embarrassing questions were asked in Parliament: "Why had the government allocated so much land to such a fly-by-night outfit? What about the rest of the undeveloped land held by the Chase people? Was it going to be forfeited to the

Crown? As long as the Americans hadn't lived up to their contract, shouldn't the land be taken away from them?"

Disgruntled residents of the area and those in search of land for development demanded some answers to those questions. Politically, the issue was a hot one and few politicians, particularly those in power, wanted to get involved. After all, the government had been instrumental in inviting the Americans to Australia; therefore it had to back us or admit it had made a mistake. And it is a cardinal rule of politics never to admit to having made a mistake.

At this juncture, Allen Chase flew to New York and met with officials of the Chase Manhattan Bank. While there were times when Allen Chase may have wished it were true, he is no relation of the Chase in Chase Manhattan. He badly needed someone to take over the grand project. He did not have a pretty picture to present in the money mart. The scheme at Esperance had been almost as great a disaster as Humpty Doo. But Australia is a long way from Manhattan, and the view from New York apparently didn't look so bad. And, of course, Allen is a superb salesman. He really demonstrated his talent when he persuaded a sophisticated group of investors on Wall Street to take over the Esperance project. These investors not only guaranteed the West Australian Government green money, but they supplied brand-new, competent management, American Factors, a giant agricultural combine which has many sugar and pineapple holdings in Hawaii.

I am sure Allen Chase was grateful to be released from the enormous responsibility of the Esperance land, because by nature he is more of a prospector than he is a developer. He gets his satisfaction from finding lucrative possibilities, organizing them, then moving on to other challenges. And indeed, not long after he divested himself of Esperance I received a telephone call from him describing another even larger and potentially more profitable proposition in the north of Australia. But that is another part of this story.

Chase kept an interest in two blocks of undeveloped land amounting to fifty thousand acres and was promised a completely developed ten-thousand-acre block by the new owners as his "price" for the original idea and groundwork with the Australian Government.

My own property played a vital part in this "sale" because by then it had proved the fruitful potential of the land, and the formula for making the sandy plain productive had been worked out and its practicality demonstrated.

Most of the original Hollywood Pioneers, their faith in Esperance shaken by the first year's failure, were content to sit and hold their property in the hope it would increase in value as the community grew. A few, aside from myself, had gone ahead with some development work. George Newton, for example. George is an experimentalist. He had chosen a low, marshy piece of land which caused him to be known around Esperance as Swamp Newton. He tried growing seeds for exotic grasses which would have a quick cash value and his venture was quite successful. Randolph Galt, a young wealthy American businessman, slowly but steadily developed his ten thousand acres along orthodox lines. Bob Cummings, Charles Correll, Rhonda Fleming, and others were content to let their land "rest" while awaiting developments.

When Chase Manhattan and American Factors came into the picture they brought a big bundle of that green stuff which is so necessary for growing grass. And certainly equally important, they brought management! From that time forward things started humming at Esperance. Almost overnight unemployment ceased; every available man was put to work. Trucks and tractors began rolling the country roads, their progress marked by plumes of dust; clearing stepped up; plows began turning over the soil; and fences laid long lines all around us. This work went on from sunup to sundown and at night the pubs, like the patrons, were loaded.

What we had flamboyantly promised when we first arrived at Esperance slowly became a reality. A superphosphate plant was built in the area and this was a real boost for the farmers. Each year it produces thousands of tons of fertilizer, and because much of the shipping and handling charges have been eliminated, the cost is reasonable. New settlers were now able to get loans to develop land and they moved in by the dozens. With the increase in population, we saw less and less of the dingoes and crows. Even the kangaroos began retreating into the bush.

The Australian kangaroo is one of nature's most hilarious jokes—a creature that looks as if he had been thought up by a cartoonist. Of all the animals of the earth, with the possible exception of the giraffe, I think the kangaroo is the most absurd looking. Surprisingly, he is also the most readily domesticated, although this spring-legged animal with the squirrel-like appearance can be very vicious if sufficiently provoked. If he doesn't like you, his powerful hind legs can pack a wicked wallop. Nevertheless, kangaroos are not antagonistic by nature and have little fear of man. They eat their share of pasture, of course, and occasionally, when they get amorous or panicky, they knock down a fence. But by and large they are gentle and sometimes have become station pets.

Kangaroos carry their babies in a pouch, but the offspring are not born in the pouch. The babies are born immature, undeveloped, and incomplete only a few weeks after gestation and are very tiny, only about an inch long. With an instinct that is truly uncanny, the naked embryo leaves the womb, crawls up through its mother's fur, and enters the sanctuary of the belly pouch. There it attaches itself strongly to one of the teats. In fact, the baby clamps its mouth onto the teat with such firmness that it cannot be pulled away without rupturing its lips. To make that journey from the womb to the pouch generally takes about half an hour, and it is difficult to see how the mother helps her baby in any way. The baby kangaroo, called a joey, continues to use its mother's pouch as a place of refuge and as a means of transport until it is too large to fit in, usually about nine months.

In the early stages of its life, the embryo is too weak to suck milk from its mother's nipple, so the milk is forced into its mouth and throat by a natural pumping contraction of muscles in the mother's breast.

If a kangaroo gives birth to another embryo before the developing joey is out of the pouch, the new baby will attach itself to another of the mother's four teats, thus allowing the older one to suckle on his teat for several more months. As the joey grows bigger, he pops in and out of the pouch at will.

If something happens to the kangaroo embryo to prevent its reaching the pouch, another embryo will emerge and take its place in the pouch. Nature has made a cruel but practical provision to ensure that multiple marsupial births will not exceed the capacity of the mother to feed them. In the case of the marsupial cat found in Australia, which bears up to twenty kittens, only six will survive because the mother has only six nipples—another example of nature's survival-of-the-fittest law.

Adult male kangaroos are called boomers in Western Australia and adult females, flying does. It takes about four years for a male to attain adulthood and around age twelve he begins to decline into old age. The largest species of boomers attain a height of seven feet and may weigh as much as three hundred pounds. They are all muscle, bone, and sinew, but the aborigines are very fond of them as food. Does, on the other hand, mature earlier than bucks, stand no more than five feet, and will weigh on the average about eighty pounds. Does are more timid than bucks and have a somewhat different color. Being lighter in weight, does are faster than boomers, and it is common in Australia to compare any fast thing, an automobile for example, to a "blue flyer," referring to a maiden doe about eighteen months old. A blue flyer is considered the swiftest creature in the bush and some have been clocked at nearly forty miles an hour. At half-pace, kangaroos can run for twenty miles without stopping; and they can run for five miles at full speed, their hops covering as much as thirty feet.

The kangaroo is an excellent defensive fighter. Dingoes and dogs have great respect for them. It would take an exceptionally valiant, strong, and skilled dog to beat a boomer. The kangaroo will back into a corner and take on two dogs at once. Balanced on his great tail, the boomer kicks with his powerful rear legs. His feet are armed with sharp claws and I have seen dogs ripped open by a kangaroo's kick.

One of the most exciting things I have ever seen was a territorial fight between two adult male kangaroos. The bucks fight to gain or defend a particularly favored feeding area or to protect a female. Their fight preliminaries are very comical. The eyes meet and glare, the hair rises along the back of the neck, and the combatants claw at the dust while circling for advantageous positions. After these formalities have been dispensed with, the kangaroos begin sparring, ineffectively at first, estimating their adversary's strength and prowess. Then all of a sudden, as if on cue, they spring at each other simultaneously, and from then on it is a matter of life or death.

In their fighting, kangaroos combine strength with science. They take into account balance and position. They use their forearms for holding and wrestling, their hind feet to rip and slash. They sometimes use their forefeet as fists, like boxers. But principally they rear back on their huge tails and use their hind feet and legs as battering rams and eviscerators.

Most kangaroo fights have an audience, because these animals invariably travel in groups (called mobs by the Aussies). Both sexes and all ages of 'roos follow the action with such intense interest and excitement you would think they had paid for tickets and had bets on the outcome. The young bucks engage in shadow-boxing off by themselves, and the does hop about in anguished excitement. When it is all over and the conqueror has retired from the arena leaving his opponent maimed or dying on the ground, the final winners of every fight in the bush will come—those scavengers, the crows and magpies. These vultures wing in from every direction to devour the defeated warrior.

Kangaroos have enemies, too; the eagle is one of the worst. Eagles work in pairs: while one bird engages the mother kangaroo's attention, the other swoops down onto the joey she is carrying in her pouch. With the precision of a hornet numbing a spider, the eagle sinks its talons into the baby's spinal cord, paralyzing it; and with hardly a pause, the bird lifts the joey out of the pouch and flies away with it.

Kangaroos are hunted commercially for their pelts. Their skins have no sweat pores, and although the leather is very tough it feels smooth and soft, like silk. Kangaroo fur is widely used in Australia in the manufacture of fashion articles for women.

We hunt kangaroos at Esperance, not for their fur but because they are a damned nuisance. It is not too extravagant, I think, to say that 'roos seem to sense green grass from fifty to a hundred miles out. Rainstorms that move in a straight line with the precision of a regiment are characteristic of arid portions of Western Australia. Rain may fall on an area ten miles long and sixty miles wide and not moisten an acre outside that strip. Kangaroos can detect these line storms from great distances and they know that where rain is falling, green grass will spring up almost overnight. This awareness and their great speed enable 'roos to reach and strip these "oasis" areas well ahead of less sensitive man and his slow-traveling sheep and cattle. And because kangaroos are swift and prolific and because they eat our grasses, we have to get rid of them. It is a shame, too, because otherwise they are quite likable creatures in their cool and rather indifferent way.

The best time to hunt the kangaroo is at night because he is basically a nocturnal animal. I recently had occasion to check accurately the speed and endurance of a kangaroo. Four of us set out on a hunt in a "ute" (utility) pickup. Our weapons were .22-caliber rifles and one revolver. After we had gone about ten miles into the bush our headlights spotted a ruby-eyed mob of about fifteen kangaroos.

Mobs of 'roos have sentries on duty at all times. At the first scent or sound of danger the one entrusted with this responsibility stands erect, his sensitive ears and nose twitching madly to determine the nature and direction of the hazard. When he decides what and where the problem is, he thumps the ground with the powerful hind feet and emits a startling grunt—an alarm which probably means "Let's get the hell out of here!" The whole mob takes off en masse.

Alerted by their sentry and blinded by the glare of our truck's headlights, the mob of 'roos we came upon set out hop-vaulting frantically across the bumpy plain. At first they stayed to-

Kangaroos are unwelcome at Linkletter's place because they denude pasture areas and thereby cause sheep and cattle to starve.

gether but when they saw they weren't going to be able to shake us, they scattered in all directions, each one out to save his own skin.

We were eager to clock the speed of a doe, so we singled out one adult female and chased this "blue flyer" at an average speed of about thirty-three miles an hour. She was absolutely magnificent. It was a performance worthy of a beautifully trained ballerina. But it was more than a ballet—it was a dramatic dance of death. I think each of her hops must have covered twenty-five feet. And in one burst of speed, toward the end of the race, the speedometer on the bouncing Toyota pickup was clocking thirty-eight miles an hour. We didn't know it then, but she was carrying in her pouch a fully furred, almost grown baby. She kept trying to shake us, but no matter which way she veered, we followed her. And in the glare of our headlights, blocked in by the black of the night, it was an eerie and exciting contest.

In flight, the kangaroo has the stance and appearance of a downhill skier taking a series of short jumps. The doe's long, ski-like legs were like mighty, high-tempered springs, and this one had the heart of a mother lion. But every creature of the earth has a limit to its endurance, and in time she began to tire.

Her speed and grace were incredible, her courage an inspiration. But gradually her pace slowed, her hops became shorter and shorter, and finally when, exhausted, she realized the chase was all but over, she ejected her baby, thereby giving it a chance for survival. She then hopped on perhaps a hundred yards where she stopped, turned, and stood, offering herself as a sacrifice.

We took seven kangaroos that night—four does, three bucks, and three joeys. One of the babies, about half the size of my little finger, was only forty-eight hours old. It was firmly attached to one of its mother's teats. The interior of the mother's pouch was spotlessly clean and the color of pink coral.

I cannot condemn the frontier Australian for the slaughter of the kangaroo, who eats as much grass as a sheep and can starve out a whole herd if his numbers are not controlled. I don't condemn because I remember in frontier America we destroyed the passenger pigeon to the point of extinction, and the millions of buffalo that roamed from north to south down the western plains in the 1830's are now confined to small herds on reserves or used for exhibit in zoos. They, too, were pests and stood in the way of man's progress in creating a pastoral America. It is no different in Australia.

On another occasion I learned how incredibly far and high a kangaroo can leap. I had assumed that the six-foot-nine-inch wire fences of Australian cattle ranches were beyond a kangaroo's capability to clear, but I learned differently. I had been invited by George Newton and his brother Bill to witness the intelligence and mustering skill of one of their prize sheep dogs. Along with their Australian manager, Murray Polkinghorn, we drove a mile or more from the Newton homestead and stopped at a gate where several hundred Merino rams and a few Hereford cows were grazing in a fenced compound. The compound was dotted with scrub trees and bushes and the sheep were scattered among them. Murray whistled for his dog and, with nothing but a verbal command, sent him across the compound to round up the sheep and herd them to the gate.

As we watched, several of the rams broke away from the herd and cut away through the low bushes, the dog at their flying heels. Suddenly from the bushes a great male kangaroo exploded skyward and headed for a corner where several head of cattle were standing. Without altering direction or changing pace, the boomer with one great vault soared over the backs of two cows and also cleared the fence. As he disappeared into the bush the four of us mere Homo sapiens looked at each other in disbelief.

Continental Australia and Tasmania contain something over three hundred species of furred animals, about half of which are, like the great kangaroos, of the marsupial family found only in Australia. There are a few ancestral marsupials, such as the opossum, for example, found in America and other parts

Aborigine recipe: "*Take one kangaroo and a heap of hot dirt. . . .*"

of the world, but for some strange whim of nature these pouched mammals had their maximum development in the land down under. The fact that New Guinea has a preponderant marsupial population lends credence to the theory that a land bridge once existed between the two now isolated countries.

When discussing marsupials, one should not overlook the koala. I'm sure there are people in the vicinity of Disneyland who trustingly believe that Walt Disney invented this dopey, cuddly little creature which is often referred to as the Australian teddy bear. The koala is not a bear, nor is he related to the monkey, nor to the sloth with whom he shares an easy-going intimacy. The koala is a marsupial, like the kangaroo. It produces a baby less than an inch long which develops in the mother's pouch until weaned and able to move outside. Unlike the kangaroo, however, the baby koala does not return periodically to the pouch. Once weaned, it rides either on its mother's back or within her forearms, clinging to her chest. The word "darling" must have been coined for them.

The nearest-living relative to the koala is his ground-dwelling Aussie cousin, the wombat. Unlike the small koala, however, the wombat sometimes grows to about a hundred pounds in weight, and it is without doubt the most intelligent of all marsupials.

Koalas grow and live in trees, specifically the eucalyptus, and scientists know that this cute, soft, grizzly-gray little animal was living in Australia's eucalyptus trees as early as half a million years ago. Seeking no conquest, the koala made no enemies, and so it survived through the centuries until the great despoiler, the white man, came. The aborigines had lived at peace with the koala for ten thousand years, probably because the little teddy's flesh is not a tasty food. His diet of eucalyptus leaves causes his meat to have a bitter taste. But aside from this, the childlike cry of a wounded or lost koala caused the aborigines to believe that he was the reincarnation of a dead child.

It was the aborigine who gave the koala his name, which

means "I don't drink." The name is extremely apt because the koala absorbs all the water he needs from the two kinds of eucalyptus leaves on which he feeds. His diet of gum leaves is deficient in carbohydrates, fat, and proteins, so the koala must consume vast quantities of this rough food to stay alive. Good old nature has responded to his problems by providing him with an appendix very much like an intestine—it is six to eight feet in length. Before he is old enough to digest rough leaves, the baby koala lives on the processed feces dropped by its mother.

White men began destroying the koala in the early 1900's for his fur. It is estimated that more than ten million koalas were shot for their pelts during the period 1900 to 1925. Today special sanctuaries have been set aside for the koala to atone for that savagery which almost sent him into oblivion. The tailless thirty-inch koala of today bears little resemblance to his giant ancestor *(koalemus)* of the Pleistocene period. That baby tipped the scales at about half a ton, and it is difficult to visualize a tree that would sustain him. He must have lived and fed on the ground.

If you ever have the chance, as I did in Brisbane, to visit a koala "farm" and pick up one of these lovable little creatures, be sure you hold him by his forearms, which are strong and sturdy. Anyone not familiar with the animals would tend to lift them by the body, under the arms. This is wrong, because koalas have almost no rib structure, and holding them by the body compresses their diaphragm. Being unable to breathe, they begin frantically pawing the air (and their temporary host) with their sharp claws.

To leave Australia's marsupials on a good and constructive note, let me tell you that there is one, a marsupial mole, whose pouch opens backward so that while digging her way through her mole world, she will not be hamstrung by constantly filling her own pouch with earth!

CHAPTER FOURTEEN

Harvest Time in the "Clip" Joints

The manager of a station in the outback has to be much more than farmer, engineer, water conservationist, animal husbandry expert, buyer, seller, agronomist, veterinarian, and machinist. He has to be the "big daddy" of the station for all of the workers and their families. One of his most difficult tasks comes at sheep-shearing time, when he has to keep peace between the visiting "sundowners" and the regular employees, especially the jackeroos. At shearing time, he must be referee, judge, and jury in a wool-gathering free-for-all.

The word "sundowner" originally meant a hobo who dropped in at a station in hopes of getting food and shelter for a few days for doing odd jobs. He was the counterpart of that American character of yesteryear, the "grub-liner," that is, a ranch-hand-cowpuncher who drifted from one cattle outfit to another, never staying in one place for long because of an incurably itchy foot. Both the sundowner and the grub-liner would bring news of other outfits, would tell stories and occasionally sing songs, and because of this they were always welcome on the lonely plains. However, these gypsies would stay only long enough to earn a few dollars, then they'd move on, restlessly looking for something new. Today, "sundowner" has come to mean a migratory worker who arrives at a station as part of a traveling crew which performs the very skillful and backbreaking work of getting the wool off the back of the sheep.

Lambing and shearing times are the most hectic and exciting periods of the year on a sheep ranch. The homestead is aroused from its regular routine and begins to shake, rattle, and roll as the jackeroos and everyone else on the ranch are pressed into extra service of one kind or another. The visiting sundowners bring an air of excitement to the place. These nomad shearers tend to be a rough, tough, blasphemous breed full of rambunctiousness and just plain hell, a rough-and-ready element of Australian society which does a very difficult job with fierce independence.

After-work hours are for rousing, and if at the end of a long day the pubs are too far away, as they generally are, the shearers amuse themselves otherwise—with a fist or dog fight or a chase over the pastures after the rabbits and 'roos. Sundowners, who are in the employ of a general contractor, are well paid for a dirty job, are protected by a strong union, and, as a rule, work beautifully as a team. They know they are indispensable to the sheep owner; they know every syllable in the small print of their contract, and to them nothing save the contract is sacred. They are quick to criticize the boss, the owner, the cook, and anyone or anything else, and if you don't like it you can go wallop a wallaby.

A couple of days before the shearers themselves arrive, an "expert" advance man shows up at the station. It is his job to see that every care has been taken to make "the clip" a smooth one. He oils and checks the shearing machinery, gives the power supply a trial run, tests the handpieces, and sharpens the cutters. He also grinds out any hollows or irregularities in the combs. And everything he does is highly important because the speed of the shearer depends as much on his tools as on his skill.

The boss of the shearers is likely to be a flamboyant fellow whose flashy dress may include a couple of searchlight-size diamond rings. His florid face may sport a broad moustache. He is the king of the roost. And if you are in the business of

"No, no! The one in the doorway's the boss—the other's a shearer walking off 'cos there's no air conditioning!!"

raising sheep for wool, he is essential to your operation and you take great pains to treat him with nice, soft kid gloves.

The shearing shed, which stands empty most of the year, will rock with activity at shearing time and resound with the crying protest of thousands of penned sheep. The shearing board, deep in a year's dust, will become soaked with sheep grease. The powerful odors of sheep lanolin, manure, wool, tar, and strong tobacco, to say nothing of the most pungent of all, sheep dip, all blend into an overpowering miasma of animal scent.

Sheep dip is an organic phosphate which kills body lice, ticks, and other parasites to which sheep are hosts. The law requires that after a sheep has been sheared it get a good bath in the dip. While huddled in a round galvanized tin spray pen, sixty sheep at a time are hose-sprayed from overhead with this strong liquid. The sheep protest loudly while undergoing this indignity. Add their shrill cacophony to the barking of dogs, the shouting and cursing of men, and the drone of the shearing machinery and you'll get some idea of the discordant symphony which accompanies the fantastic operation of harvesting wool.

The sheep themselves—no two are exactly alike—are studies in contrasting reaction to their annual clipping. Here a matronly ewe with a rather aristocratic bearing, whose high-C bleat seems to rise above the flagrant indignity that is being done her. And there a bored old wether, who has been through this lousy business a dozen times, endures it stoically. While he does not like either the dust, the noise, the confusion, the man-handling, or the spraying, he knows that once he has been shorn of that twelve-pound mattress he is carrying around, he will feel immensely better. The wool not only keeps a sheep too warm, it houses irritating vermin, catches on thorny bushes, and picks up dirt.

Though each of the animals has his own characteristics, each also carries in his veins the blue blood of the pedigreed Merino of ancient Spain. For days the sheep have been penned and driven and hounded by men and dogs, and now, once through this ordeal, ahead of them are long months of peace and security and contentment in green pasture. After the shearing they will go back to the paddocks and begin the miraculous process of growing more blankets and carpets and sweaters.

A good shearer will take the wool off a sheep's back in about five minutes, and he will shear on the average about seventy to one hundred sheep a day. The contractor is paid 44¢ for each sheep that is sheared, and the shearer gets the major portion of this. A shearer will earn perhaps $20 or more a day, an especially handsome wage in Australia, earned the hard way. The average Australian wage is between $58 and $62 a week, although special skills range upward from that. A carpenter, for example, receives a minimum wage of $52 a week. Low as these wages are in comparison with those paid in the United States, Australians find that their earnings have compensatory depth in spending power. With reasonable thrift, the average Aussie worker manages to own a car, a refrigerator, a washing machine, perhaps a television set, and is paying for his home while supporting a wife and two children. Meat and vegetables are cheap and plentiful, and a man can buy a good suit for $40 or $50. One of the best indications of the prosperity level in Western Australia is the fact that Perth and other larger towns are fringed with substantial homes, most of them occupied and owned by people in the medium wage bracket. It is difficult to find what could be accurately termed a slum anywhere in Australia.

Though he makes a lot of money, the handsomely paid shearer is quick to blow his earnings. The adage "easy sheared, easy shorn" fits him very well. The work is seasonal, of course. The good pickings do not last long, and after the shearing season is over the average shearer will spend the lot of his earnings in the nearest string of pubs and go off penniless and cheerful to the bend of a billabong, an Australian name for the pools formed by backwaters. There he will camp and "make do" until shearing time comes around again.

For our shearers at shearing time we must have separate and special sleeping quarters on the ranch and we also supply them

Gentlemen shearers off on a spree: *"Chuck us out when the cheques cut out, Mister Barman!"*

with a separate kitchen and cook. Furthermore, their food had better be good, plentiful, and to their liking; if it isn't, there's sure to be trouble. After a day's work at the shearing board, the sundowners retire to their bunkhouse and guzzle rum-brandy which, wherever they work, must be in plentiful supply. While they drink the liquor, they wolf down unbelievable amounts of food. We slaughter a sheep a day to supply food for the shearers and the other employees on the place. A majority of Australians demand their daily "stike an' aigs," whether or not the "stike" is beef or a mutton chop.

After supper, some of the shearers play euchre for plugs of chewing tobacco. Others lounge in the bunks which line the walls and sing to the accompaniment of a concertina. The beer and rum-brandy keep making the rounds, and chances are good that before the night is out a couple of blokes will get into some kind of an argument. A popular subject for debate is which man can shear the most sheep in a given time. This braggadocio often turns into a lively fistfight. Encouraged by their mates, the battlers go at it hammer and tongs until they are exhausted, then they shake hands and concede that the question is pretty academic. By the next morning they go off arm in arm to the shearing board to put through their daily tallies of sheep.

The shearing season in Australia relates to the weather cycle, the same as in the United States. In America, shearing starts in springtime on the Mexican-American border and moves northward toward the Canadian border as the weather moderates. In Australia, the shearing season moves ahead of the rains which begin in the northern tropic belt and move southward toward the south pole and the cooler climate.

The work is never regular, though. Some farmers prefer to shear at one time, some another. And, actually, a few weeks one way or the other doesn't make any difference, particularly in a temperate climate where one season merges into another. However, distances between sheep stations are so great that shearers usually confine themselves to one general area.

Generally speaking, the Australian "clip" is done during July, August, and September, but at Linkletter's Place we shear in late October. Some shearers may have enough work to last them for six months, and every shearing team will have a schedule of timed engagements ahead of it. For this reason and because they get paid by the piece (or fleece), shearers are always in a hurry. That's why everything must run smoothly for them. The sheep must be brought in a constant line to the shearing shed, and everybody prays that the wool will not be rain-dampened or soaking wet. At the first sign of rain, the union rule books are pulled out; an estimate of the precipitation is made, and the "steward" decides whether or not the men work that day!

There is just no scene like the shearing shed at the height of the action. The shearer almost seems to be performing a ritualistic dance, maneuvering a sheep, like a partner, into various positions. With controlled movement of his arms and feet the shearer, to the accompaniment of the whir of hand-held clippers, strips away the sheath of wool that clothes the animal. With dexterous strokes in rapid succession the wool is removed from the sheep's belly, throat, neck, sides and tail. As the sheep exits via a chute, a roustabout, responding to a call of "wool away!," rushes in to gather up the fleece and place it on a "wool-rolling" table. There burrs and stains are trimmed from the fleece which is then placed on a "piece-pickers" table for sorting and grading. As a new sheep enters the area, the ballet resumes; the same movements being repeated with hypnotic regularity until a whistle blows signaling time for a "smoko"—the equivalent of our coffee break. The cook provides tea and cakes, and the din of relaxed conversation succeeds the music of the vibrating clippers.

Meanwhile, the anxious owner stands by to keep an eye on apprentice shearers, who, through clumsiness, may cut the sheep. If an unskilled man bloodies too many sheep, the owner will demand that he be removed from the shearing line.

Keeping these rough, tough, and rousing shearers in line requires firmness, tact, and absolute fairness. Indeed, to maintain harmony between the shearers and the other ranch employees is enough to tax even the most skilled arbiter. Things can get explosively out of hand. Fortunately, for our place John Hagon is more than up to the challenge. He knows all the tricks of the trade and has invented a few of his own. He has learned to be a patient listener, which is a prime requirement for any station manager. And watching him handle one ticklish situation after another, including a few between wives on the station, I think he must have been born a diplomat. He is not only judge, jury, and gentle executioner, but also general conciliator, chaperone, and social director for his little community.

In his role of social director, John originated the annual New Year's Eve party at the then-quiet shearing shed, and this has turned out to be an institution at Esperance.

It all began when the Parents' League needed to raise funds to purchase a few extras for the school. John suggested a charity party, an idea that was enthusiastically adopted. Invitations went out to all of the neighbors, which means those within twenty-five to forty miles. Fifty or sixty responded that first year and they had what we Americans used to call a hoedown. From Esperance, John recruited a rousing three-piece orchestra which, if it wasn't great in musicianship, certainly played with tremendous spirit. There was dancing, beer-drinking, and a dozen participation games for homemade prizes, and then there was more beer-drinking.

In most places a party is just a party—food, drink, and casual companionship. But in Australia's outback, it is a very special and precious event. Consider the distances which separate neighbors, the long periods of isolation, the demanding work which fills every day seven days a week, and you can understand how a party on a sheep station in the Esperance area has much more significance than a party in Beverly Hills. Persons who may know one another only by voice over the telephone or radio have an opportunity to meet face to face and share their problems and pleasures.

Last year more than two hundred attended the Hagons' New

Year's Eve party, and the proceeds have gone to finance a number of other social activities for the benefit of the community. In that outback shearing shed there were bone china plates, saucers and cups, damask napkins, and food flown in from Perth. The ladies were dressed in their fanciest homemade dresses and the men were spruced-up almost beyond recognition.

This annual party at our place brings together ranch owners, managers, and overseers, people who are extremely knowledgeable about their work and their land. Despite the fact that they are of varying economic status, education, and experience, it is a classless society. And classlessness is an important facet of the Australian character.

The people in the outback are unbelievably good-hearted, hardworking, and healthy. They are largely unsophisticated in the urban sense but they take on an air of honest sophistication at the Hagons' New Year's Eve party. They never try to put on false airs, but at the same time within their own frame of reference they have a genuine appreciation for the "amenities."

The ranch grew and prospered and its fame spread. And now to John's many other duties was added a new responsibility. He became perforce a greeter and tour guide for visiting firemen and officials. As word of our place spread across Australia and to the United States, visitors to Western Australia began asking the way to it; they wanted to see what was going on. Farmers, agronomists, investors, and just plain open-mouthed tourists began to arrive unannounced and unheralded. Some had driven out from Esperance, but most of these visitors came from Perth, 500 miles away, and not a few from Melbourne and Sydney, 2,500 miles away. They assumed that when they arrived their interest would be appreciated and someone would show them around the place. For a while, Hagon extended such courtesies, as any hospitable Australian would. The visitors in every case had come a long way and he felt obligated to entertain them to some extent. But in time this chore became a nuisance. He discovered he was "herding"

The Hagons' New Year's Eve Party.

more tourists than sheep. The demands on his time became unreasonable. Regretfully, because running Linkletter's Place is a round-the-clock job that permits no time out for casual sociability, we had to erect a No Trespassing sign over the big entrance gate.

CHAPTER FIFTEEN

I Reckon It Could Be Worse

When I began to see how well things were developing at Esperance, I purchased a second plot of ten thousand acres several miles away from my place. This I gave to my five children and five grandchildren, a thousand acres each. I thus linked the Linkletter family firmly to Western Australia and to its future history. Then I turned around and leased this new farm back from the kids, and John Hagon and I began to develop it into a joint sheep and cattle operation, known as the Condingup Pastoral Company. Following the same procedure we had used on my original plot, John chained and burned a thousand acres a year. The following year the cleared area was plowed, harrowed, and planted. We used newly proven varieties of pasture grasses and clovers which produced even better and more sustained feed. We were learning to take advantage of the seasons in breeding the livestock. Costs had gone down dramatically since the days of 1957 when supplies were so far away and roads bumped our vehicles to pieces in a few short years.

Thanks to the new superphosphate plant, we can now buy fertilizer at a tremendous saving over what we had to pay in the old days. When the new school was built on the Condingup townsite, the old Linkletter schoolhouse became a study center and demonstration lab for those budding young farmers, the jackeroos.

When I was gathering material for this book, I asked John how much revenue his own place was producing. He wrote:

In 1966 the gross income from my station was around $10,000, 40 percent of which went toward operating costs. The balance went into development. My farm's gross income for 1967 should be approximately $15,000 and production costs should be about 45 percent of the gross. The profit will also go into further development. . . .

We call the place Greendale and income from it should increase about 20 percent a year for the next three or four years, until the existing pastured area of 2,200 acres is fully productive. When the total area of 4,200 acres is in full production it will carry approximately twelve to fifteen thousand sheep and proportionate numbers of cattle, with possibly some cereals as well. The gross income then should be about $70,000 to $85,000 and the net should be about 50 percent of the gross.

The way I have developed my assets is different in some ways from what other young men who came to Esperance with limited capital have done. Things have been a little easier for me, as I had had the advantage of rewarding employment and financial assistance, where others have suffered the ups and downs of the contracting world.

Of my 4,200 acres, 3,140 were allocated by the Western Australian Lands Department in October 1956; I purchased the rest in 1965. The allocated land cost fifty cents an acre, and the land purchased later in a more improved condition cost from eight to ten dollars an acre. The two parcels join. I have a man running my farm on a contract basis. Actually, he looks after the stock and I have other major work carried out on contract. From 1968 I will have a man on the property full time.

My position here on Linkletter's Place allows me little time for my own station, but from the income there and from my job here I have enough to pay someone else to do the necessary work. We live on my salary, and my share of the gross income here goes into developing Greendale. With our beach *house in Esperance, our present assets amount to a figure slightly in excess of $155,000. They have increased by $50,000 during the last two years.*

Generally, whatever John does on our place and the kids' station, he does on his own place, and vice versa. He is responsible for everything that takes place on 26,000 acres of highly populated (with sheep) land. You know he's got to be a very busy man.

A good way to get a true picture of the operation at Linkletter's is to read another of John Hagon's letters. While letter-writing cannot help being an onerous chore for him, he keeps me remarkably well informed on the station's progress. In this way, although he makes the day-to-day decisions, he can look to me for decisions on extraordinary expenditures and for overall policy and budgets. I quote from one of his most recent missives:

Dear Mr. Linkletter: There are times when one has a stretch of work a mite high, both inside the office and out in the field, and then one has to "skimp" on time a little to try and catch up. Letter-writing takes time and time in these parts is in short supply. General labor and contractors can be so unreliable that we find ourselves doing work which was planned for a contractor. Inasmuch as the contractor didn't show up on the agreed date, we had to bring our staff in to do the work and this put us behind in other sectors. A case in point: Just after you were here last October, we had to sack our German cook when she became too slovenly. And in the interim before we found a new cook for the jackeroos, we had to have one of them do the cooking. About that time another jackeroo was conscripted into the army, so we were two men down, and right at shearing time.

My main problem is that I have to be everything from office boy to plumber to manager. I do not mind this at all, but I must say that it is the office work which usually has to wait, because developmental and production work just cannot wait without considerable expense.

My day starts around 6:30 a.m. and I am usually home

around 7:30 p.m. It takes about ten phone calls to get any sort of contractor on the job, so I usually am at the telephone from about the time I get home until it is time to go to bed. Of course there is a certain amount of other organizing to do as well. We select our tasks by priority and try to be well organized, and we cut short those items which do not have a lasting effect.

I am thankful that you take a real interest in the place. It is good and comforting to know you treat this property as something more than just an investment.

Jenny and the children went to our beach house in Esperance for a "break" January 17. I followed a few days later and worked from there. Angela started school last week at Condingup, which has grown from seven pupils when the school opened in 1961 to about forty-five this year. There are two teachers at the school now. How is that for population growth? Better than the lambing percentage—but not for long, we hope.

I am looking forward to a prosperous year. We have a very good staff and with the new jackeroos arriving we should be able to keep up with the work, provided they all measure up to their work. Our sectionalization of the property is working well. Our new man, Peter Crosby, who has been with us for six months now, is doing a wonderful job and is the best man we ever had. He runs his own section and is foreman of the jackeroos. He says he loves it here, so we hope he continues for some years. This property has developed into something more than just a run-of-the-mill place with a few sheep and cattle. Our breeding programs, Merino stud, jackeroo training system, and enterprise costing system require people with technical training, and more important, they have to be of the correct type when the training and guidance of young men is involved.

Three of the new jackeroos have arrived. Two from Western Australia and one from southern Australia—the other new one arrives on March 25, from Victoria. The last has spent two years at Agricultural College there, so he should have the makings.

Harry Berry, who has been with us for a little over three years, is leaving us to return to his home district near Perth to take up the management of a dairy farm. He has been a good man as a sectional manager and I am disappointed to lose him but we should be able to find another man to fill his position.

The high density stocking trials are going well and I am absolutely sure they will be quite successful. There still seems to be plenty of feed for them—even in the paddock where we rely only on winter-growing species such as annual clover and grasses. In the trial areas, where we have established Lucerne, the sheep are going into green grasses and clover about six to nine inches high. Under a normal set stocking method of about four or five sheep to the acre, they would eat the Lucerne right out; but we are giving the grass sixty-three days between grazings, and this gives it plenty of time to recover. I don't know whether you have a front lawn now [I have moved to a penthouse apartment] *but imagine what it would look like if you hadn't had it cut for sixty-three days!*

We sold 207 bales of wool in late January for an average price per pound of 52.07¢. With the other 28 bales of oddments sold in the same sale the average was 47.6 per pound. The remaining 350-odd bales were sold this last week and I am happy to say that the market was up by 2½ to 5 percent over the previous sale. When the details come in from the broker I will send them on to you. Our gross proceeds for 235 bales sold in the January sale was $35,937, and the net (less cost of transportation and selling) was $33,090.44.

My trip to South Australia was very successful. All the sheep purchased were mated to lamb during April, May, and June. I was pleased with the quality and we should land them here for an average of about ten dollars per head. The sheep will be coming in between late February and mid-March.

There is one important point which I would like you to consider just as soon as you can. Although we cleared some fourteen hundred acres of country on the Condingup property late last year, I feel we should not *proceed with the burning and ploughing until next year [1968] and the seeding to pasture would then be carried out in 1969. With our increased stocking rates and holding capabilities on the older pasture, we are going to find that we will be short of sheep again; and also we will have to sell some sheep as they will be getting too old for us to keep profitably. If we can consolidate for two years (1967 and 1968) before seeding more land to pasture, we will be in a better position to seed even larger areas to pasture and thereby complete development by about the same time. Also the scientists have developed a new clover which is absolutely free from any toxic substance. The seed will not be available in quantity for a couple of years. Would you give me an answer on this just as soon as you can so I can plan my program accordingly.*

Yours sincerely,
John Hagon

Section managers on our place are paid $60 a week, and the section manager who has additional responsibilities is paid $74. Regular hands are paid from $45 to $52 a week. All have to supply their own groceries, although meat produced on the property is supplied to the employees at 5¢ a pound. Living accommodations and milk are free.

The incentive program which we have had on trial for the last two years, and which seems to be working out well, is based on a point system. It works like this:

We allocate four points for each sheep on hand, including natural increase, at the end of the financial year. With one hundred points valued at two dollars, this means a bonus allocation of eight cents per head. For cattle we allocate forty points for each natural increase but nothing for adult cattle on hand. The difference in point allocation between sheep and cattle is because we run about ten sheep to every cow and produce about ten lambs to every calf. We allocate one and a half points for every bushel of wheat harvested, one point for every bushel of barley, and one half point for every bushel of oats. For deaths or losses of livestock from any cause, we deduct the average value in relation to production.

Take a hypothetical year:

	Points
10,000 sheep (4 points each)	40,000
100 cattle, natural increase only (40 points each)	4,000
4,000 bushels of wheat (1½ points)	6,000
1,000 bushels of barley (1 point)	1,000
5,000 bushels of oats (½ point)	2,500
Total points to be allocated	53,500
Less:	
400 sheep dead from all causes (minus 40 points each)	16,000
2 cattle dead (minus 200 points each)	400
Total points deducted	16,400
Total points for bonus allocation	37,100
100 points equals two dollars:	
Total Bonus	$742

We give this bonus at the end of the fiscal year only to those who play an important part in and have the best effect on efficient and harmonious production. In 1966 we gave the bonus to section managers only.

It costs us $2.50 to produce a sheep and another 60¢ to raise it for a year. It costs 44¢ to shear a sheep, and to ship and sell its wool costs 4¢ a pound. Tax on the land is 10¢ an acre per year, and at the present time we are raising four sheep to the acre.

If you add our costs you will find that to produce and raise a sheep for a year and to shear and sell its wool costs us $3.68. For that wool we get this year $4.70, so you see we are making more than 20 percent profit. And even considering the cost of the land, I am making better than 15 percent per year on my investment at Esperance.

I am immensely pleased, of course, by John's performance.

It is a great satisfaction to watch young people fulfill their promise. I placed my faith in him and he has never failed me. He has planned, budgeted, and put into effect work that has wrought a miracle. From what at one time had been considered wasteland he has created a garden that will go on producing for decades to come.

John has written to me:

> *Because of my ten-year association with this property, I have a personal feeling toward it. I think of it and run it as if it were my own. While I am aware it is not mine, I doubt if even you could feel more pride in it than I do. You supplied the "trigger" [money] and were the main contributor in establishing the bond of confidence that exists between us. Today Linkletter's Place is an established and developing business valued at not less than $1 million and the less developed younger Linkletter's property, based on local prices, is worth $300,000—only a third of its potential value.*

On occasion, when I take a jeep and bounce to the top of Condingup Mountain, I experience a thrill unique in my eventful life. No matter how often I go up there, I get a buoyant inexpressible feeling of achievement. Gazing over that vast agricultural empire I am aware that I have been instrumental in helping to pioneer a new and important area of the world and I am aware that it will be important to mankind as long as there is a world. Blended with the satisfaction is the feeling of wonder at the miracle that has been accomplished with effort, imagination, and money. We have succeeded in transforming a desert wasteland into a productive wool and meat factory. Consider me, a city boy who has never grown so much as a geranium in a window box and feel as I feel the pride of having put my green stamp on ground which stretches for so many miles it meets the blue sky. And the last time I stood there on Condingup, it occurred to me that along with the change in the land, I myself had been changed. To an extent that I had never expected, I had been fulfilled. Looking out over the homes, the paddocks, the work sheds, and the sea of green pasture dotted with forty thousand head of sheep and one thousand head of cattle, I felt the emotions any successful man must feel, an integral part of it all. I felt a oneness that can be experienced only when you have helped to create something substantial that is beneficial to mankind.

Visiting Esperance today, it is hard to believe what has happened in the last decade. After almost a century of dormancy and uncertainty the district has turned into a bountiful arcadia producing wool and meat and grain. There is no uncertainty about its future anymore. Those acres which just a little while ago were barren have been brought into productivity and will serve man for generations to come. What a few short years ago was considered wasteland is now truly a land of milk and honey.

Presently in the Esperance area there are about a million acres in various stages of development, of which some 200,000 are in cereals. The region carries about 700,000 sheep and 25,000 cattle. The increase in the sheep population has been phenomenal. In March–April 1964, there were 420,000 sheep in the district. A year later the figure was 650,000. Stock numbers in 1972 are estimated at 2 million sheep and 60,000 cattle. And agricultural experts predict that by the end of this century, the sheep population in the district will number 10 million.

The productive capacity of the land is tremendous because of the climatic conditions more than the fertility of the soil. Thanks to the mild southern-California, Mediterranean-like climate, almost anything can be grown here, just as Allen Chase told the natives when first we came. The coolest it gets, even in wintertime, is well above freezing, so there is no cessation of growth the year around. The thermometer in midsummer rarely climbs above eighty-five or ninety degrees, and there is the well-spaced rainfall—twenty-six inches a year near the coast and thirteen inches inland, most of it spread over an eight-month period.

Growing crops under natural rainfall, providing there is enough, is the very best way. And at Esperance the finest seed for cereals, linseed, and the forage grasses and legumes are

A desert wasteland has been transformed into productive acres, feeding sheep and cattle.

being successfully grown. Last year over two thousand tons of subclover seed were harvested in the district, and per acre the production was much better than comparable growth in California, Oregon, or Washington. While one has to add practically everything in the way of minerals to the light sandy soil, there are few weeds, insects, or diseases that seriously affect the crops.

Five hundred new access roads are in development or have been completed, and other road projects are being laid out.

Yes, almost all of the things we promised the natives would come to pass, have come to pass. The Esperance fertilizer works, opened in 1964, was built at a cost of three million dollars and is the most modern in the southern hemisphere. A bulk grain terminal has been completed and a slaughtering plant will be in operation soon. Esperance harbor has been dredged to a depth of thirty-two feet, and a new berth has been built to serve ships of twenty thousand tons. And the town itself is thriving.

Aside from its promising pastoral and agricultural future, the Esperance area and the inland section served by its port show great promise of productive mineral development. Gold, silver, and pyrites, used for the production of superphosphates, are plentiful and continue in heavy production, and new copper sources have been brought into production.

It is my opinion that in another fifteen to twenty years new techniques and procedures will make the Esperance district one of the richest agricultural areas in all of Australia if not the world. The potential of the land will not stop at four or five sheep to the acre, but with cropping and the proper management I think it can support, without irrigation, up to six and maybe eight sheep to the acre. I don't believe such rich production has been sustained on a large scale anywhere else in the world.

CHAPTER SIXTEEN

Our Own Little Beach . . . About Sixty Miles of Ocean Front

With things going so well at Esperance, I was in a receptive mood when Allen Chase called and asked if I would be interested in a cattle station on Western Australia's north coast.

"About a million acres are available," he said blithely, "and the place can be bought for about ten cents an acre."

"Great," I said warily, "don't need to wrap it up; I'll take it with me."

"I'm not joking," he said earnestly. "It's between Broome and Port Hedland. There are sixty miles of beach front without a human footprint and the property runs inland to an unexplored desert for forty miles."

I think it was the sixty miles of beach front that hooked me. That and the no-footprints. Beach-front property in southern California, where I live, sells for two and three thousand dollars a front foot, and while land along the Timor Sea is not comparable to that in Newport Beach, it has to be a bargain at ten cents an acre. Then, too, if I ever wanted to get away from it all, the place Allen was describing seemed the ideal place to go. So I followed my acquisitive instinct: I told him to count me in and I'd bring my own man Friday.

Others from California in this new syndicate included, besides myself and Chase, the former Texas oilman, Jack Wrather,

Irate sunbather: *"Bloody progress! There was a time when you could have the eighty-mile beach to yourself!!"*

who now operates hotels, resorts, "Lassy," and Muzak sound system. His wife is former movie star Bonita Granville. The Schwabacher brothers, Jack and Al, investment bankers and ranchers, went in on the scheme, too. John Brown Cook, a newly arrived Hollywood industrialist and part-time magician, completed the syndicate.

Actually the parcel at Anna Plains, which is about 1,500 miles north and east of Esperance, turned out to be only 970,000 acres, take or leave a rod or two. It lies halfway between Port Hedland and Broome, these towns being separated by about 370 miles of rough road.

Broome is the most Asian township in Australia. It was once a thriving center for pearl fishing and was largely inhabited by Japanese and Malays who used it as a base of operations in the Indian Ocean. The waters off this part of Australia have the world's richest pearling beds, and for years Broome was the renowned capital of the pearling industry. It supplied 80 percent of the world's pearls and nacre. Nacre is the mother-of-pearl used in the manufacture of buttons, costume jewelry, and novelties. Today men still dive for the precious gems at Broome, and the production of cultured pearls is a growing industry there.

The Japanese originated the cultured pearl technique and have become masters of it, but pearls produced in the waters off Broome, due to the abundance of nacre there, have proved to be superior to the cultured pearls of Japan. The Broome pearls vary in size up to eighteen millimeters in diameter and some are worth up to five thousand dollars each.

Northwest Australia was the region where European settlers first faced severe opposition from the aborigines, who fiercely resented being dispossessed of their lands. Reprisals on both sides led to much brutality and the situation was made worse by the Europeans "teaching the natives a lesson" with whip, boot, and bullet. The situation was very like the American frontier in the latter part of the eighteenth and early part of the nineteenth centuries.

As a result of these skirmishes between the European whites

and the native blacks, the government in an attempt to solve an awkward problem decreed that station owners had to hire aborigines and thereby bring them into the community. And although the station owners did this, for a number of years they felt very insecure. Not only were they greatly outnumbered by the aborigines, who often stole their stock and killed their drovers, but they were separated from one another by vast distances.

Broome has that look of mellowed decay one associates with tropical sea towns. During The Dry, from March to December, days are hot and sultry; during The Wet, from December to March, they're steamily humid. As in Darwin, the houses in Broome are built of galvanized metal on stilts; and, as in Darwin, the stilts are designed to raise the town's floors above the onslaught of interminable termites and also to allow cooling breezes to circulate under the houses. Hinged window shutters can be dropped against the deluges or raised to provide shade from the searing sun. Sandy streets wind away from a paved central artery where there is a pearl shop, the post office, a few other government buildings, and a huge general store which provides everyone with food, clothing, hardware, and gossip. People from the outback come here for supplies and take away stores sufficient to last them three or four months. Their land-rovers, Toyotas, jeeps, and trucks line the main drag. The polyglot populace is made up of a heterogeneous collection of people; besides the Malays and the Japanese, there are the English, the Chinese, the Filipinos, and various combinations, to say nothing of the aborigines. Dusty aborigine children stand about full of shyness, curiosity, and the hope that someone will treat them to an ice-cream cone.

The various nonwhite races were allowed to inhabit this far-north pearling port in the old days, despite Australia's otherwise rigidly enforced white-only policy, because pearling was the fifth largest exporting industry in the country, and the occupation was considered too perilous and uncongenial for white men.

Licentiousness, carousing, and fighting were the order of the day in the early times in Broome, and it became known as one of the world's most dangerous and wicked towns. It is much more circumspect today, but it still could not be called a model of morality. Now the principal diversions are dancing in the hotel's patio, the evening swill at the saloon, fishing from the municipal pier, and an occasional rodeo. The pier is new and the townspeople are proud of it. I was taken on a tour and looked down into the turquoise water of Roebuck Bay upon a multitude of listlessly floating tub-sized jellyfish. Each of these poisonous creatures trailed a network of dangerous feeding tentacles. I fished and caught a bright silver perch, but I didn't go swimming!

During the cyclone season everything in Broome is cinched down. Cyclonic storms have done tremendous damage over the years, particularly to the pearling industry. In 1908 a cyclone drowned some fifty deckhands and divers when it swept them off the luggers and washed them ashore among the mangroves.

The first time I visited our new cattle station at Anna Plains, I took a jeep ride along the forty-mile beach frontage that forms the western ocean boundary. We had hardly started over the shell-littered sand when a great flock of black and white gulls rose from their feeding areas ahead and, banking in a returning circle, became a fast-moving cloud sweeping across the early morning sun. Such easy escape was not so simple for the legions of mud crabs which scurried before us, clattering across the heaps of shells. They were the size of an adult's hand and had emerged in countless thousands from their burrows in the beach silt to feed where the tide had receded. Their unlikely, side-gliding shapes blackened the sand for hundreds of yards—one of the most extraordinary sights I have ever seen. And with thousands of them retreating frantically before us, I, of course, wanted a picture. So the driver stopped the jeep and ran across the gently sloping beach to turn the crabs before they could reach the waterline. He easily outran the awkward creatures, and in concert, like a band of milling sheep, they turned back toward the jeep and my camera. Realizing then the new danger of entrapment, the crab army suddenly performed a miracle. As if on command, while I was trying to focus the camera, their ranks came to an abrupt halt and they began to dig in. In a matter of seconds they completely disappeared, swallowed up by the sand. It was as if I had dreamed the whole scene.

During that fascinating excursion, we came upon thousands of masquerading hermit crabs. They occupy a zone between the shell dumps of high tide and the grassed dunes, where kangaroo tracks intermingle with those of the gull. I went to pick up a twirl of brown-mottled shell only to have it suddenly move away. Beneath its shining, sunproof hatch was a hermit crab. Encumbered as it was, I had little difficulty capturing the little fellow; but it was not without considerable difficulty that I managed to extract it from its adopted home. I tossed its shell ten or twelve feet away and released the naked creature to see what it would do. At once it began a frantic search for another abode. In great haste it tried and abandoned one shell after another. Some were too large, some were too small, and others were occupied. I followed as the frightened little guy continued its anxious search. Suddenly and with almost comical relief, it came upon its previous home, which it recognized at once. In an instant it had backed into the shell, twisted, turned, and shrugged into its deepest contour. Wanting no more of me, the crab, shell and all, burrowed into the sand and slammed its front door, with not even a fare-thee-well or a go-to-hell.

As I prodded about, I found that almost every discarded shell, other than the scallop variety, was serving as a home for a hermit. They ranged in size from a dime to a dollar, and there were two or three hermit giants, possibly the kings and queens, moving about with four-inch shells on their backs. As they scurried in search of larger homes to contain their growing bodies, I was struck by the continual quarreling among them. Maybe that's why they are called crabs. There is always a screwball in any society, even crabs, and the one I saw was carrying a bright branch of pink coral as if it were a protest banner. Probably an anarchist.

The low cape toward which we had been driving for thirty miles slowly came into sharper focus. This thrust of land is no higher than ten feet, but it breaks the pattern of the sea and the sand. As we approached we could see clinging to the coral promontory the exposed roots of mangrove trees. These proved to be covered with small living oysters clinging in clusters above the waterline. Thick-shelled and very difficult to open, each contained a copper-flavored morsel no larger than an English penny.

Standing on the point of the promontory, I looked across the incoming surf to the aquamarine water beyond. With each successive swell the amber, dome-shaped bodies of tentacled jellyfish were silhouetted. An enormous black body rose to the surface and I saw the serpentine head of a gigantic sea turtle as it came up for air; having filled his lungs, he disappeared again in the curve of a wave.

Shells and driftwood were strewn on either side of me. I picked up a piece of cuttlefish bone from a windrow five feet deep. It is the substance bird-lovers place in the cages of canaries and parakeets. And even as I stood there a flock of tufted linnet-like birds came in from the scrub with a chorus of cries and began pecking away at pieces of the bone.

But one of the most intensely interesting aspects of Australian marine life is the maternal role played by certain male fish in this area. Take the percelle for an example. Similar to some American spiders, the females of this fish, after laying eggs in a sheltered cove, abandon them. The incubation of the eggs and the rearing of the offspring is left to the male. Once the female percelle has done her job the male scoops the eggs up in his mouth and carries them about until they incubate and hatch. This is a tiresome paternal obligation and involves complete dedication and a long period of uninterrupted fasting. The father dares not open his mouth until the babies have been hatched. Even then his responsibility does not end, because the fingerlings which cruise beside him rush back into the sanctuary of his mouth at any sign of threat or danger.

Most extraordinary of these paternal fish, though, is the overly dedicated kurtas. The male of this ilk possesses a bony hook which projects from his forehead. This put-upon and long-suffering fellow will tread around while his charming mate lays her eggs. These will come in two bunches, each about the size of a golf ball, and will be connected by a thin but tough thread. Once the eggs are deposited, the male rushes in, scoops them up on his hook, and swims away, a bundle of eggs dangling from either side of his head. He will continue to carry and guard these pouches of eggs until they hatch. Inasmuch as the eggs are attractive morsels to other varieties of fish, the male kurtas spends a good portion of the incubation time fleeing from one shelter to another in defense of his precious picnic burden. It is indeed a strange world!

But to get back to the cattle station at Anna Plains. The people from whom we bought the property were not certain how many cattle there were on it. Guesses ranged from 17,000 to 25,000. In purchasing the station we had agreed to buy the cattle at so much a head—a matter of simple arithmetic—but, as a matter of simple deduction, we had to know how many head there were. The big question was how to count them. They were scattered over a thousand square miles, and while they moved in herds, as a rule, and stuck fairly close to the water holes, it was a long-drawn-out job trying to get a count by jeep and on horseback over an area of 900,000 acres. Farther north in the Kimberley mountains we had another million-acre cattle station and were faced with the same problem of getting an accurate cattle count. The Dunham Station is deeply cut with canyons and even the rugged jeep was overmatched.

We solved the problem by hiring a helicopter. Counting cattle by helicopter may not be the most accurate technique ever devised, but it was the only way we could get an approximation in a short time.

As our chopper whirled its way over a Kimberley ridge

above a canyon dotted with ghost gums, we spotted a herd of very odd-looking beasts. They sure didn't look like cattle. "Hey," I shouted to the pilot, "look over there; I'd swear it was a herd of camels!"

He nodded.

"You mean it really is?"

He nodded again.

"Let's go have a look!" I hollered.

The pilot banked the whirlybird and we started down.

Camels were brought to Australia from central Asia to help man conquer the staggering, waterless distances of the continent. Without this marvelously strong, patient, and tractable animal, many of the inner reaches in the old days would not have been accessible at all. Camel caravans driven by Afghans crisscrossed Australia for years, carrying merchandise and supplies to those who labored in the outback. They also brought in their saddlery seeds of some of the worst weed pests in all of Australia.

(I pause at this juncture to bow symbolically in the direction of those ruminant quadrupeds, the dromedary and the Bactrian, for if ever an animal deserves a niche in heaven, the camel certainly does. Despite his ornery disposition, he has done more than his share, not only in Australia but in dry lands throughout the world, to further the progress of mankind.)

After the automobile and the airplane came to Australia, camels became obsolete and their owners turned them loose to forage for themselves. Despite the desolation of the outback North where they wandered, and the scarcity of water, some of them have managed to survive.

"I'd like to see how tame they are!" I shouted to the pilot, and imagined myself riding sidesaddle on a captured camel down Hollywood Boulevard.

As we got close to them, the camels, alarmed by our unfamiliar bird, fled from us, led by a gigantic, one-humped bull. We hovered just above the ground and followed the beasts. When they reached the end of a canyon and could go no farther, the bull stopped, and with the cows and calves assembled behind him under a ghost gum, stood his ground belligerently.

I asked the pilot if it would be all right to land. He shrugged and started to put the helicopter down. Even with the noise and the clouds of dust the chopper created, the old bull was not intimidated. As soon as the helicopter touched the ground he charged.

Instantly the pilot gunned the engine and the rotors lifted us up again, beyond the bull's reach. He could have done us serious damage, and neither the pilot nor I had any hankering to walk. It was a good twenty miles back to headquarters. Having chased us away, the bull went majestically back to his harem.

We saw cattle all over that black country, many of them scrawny as goats. They live on spinafex, buffo, and kapok grasses. The seed of the buffo, interestingly enough, was one of those brought in the padding of camel saddles more than a hundred years ago. Somehow it got started and now it is important to the cattle industry.

Many of the cattle we rounded up that first time at both Dunham and Anna Plains Stations were clean-skinned; that is, they were unbranded. This troubled me at first, but I was told that a sort of *quid pro quo,* give-and-take kind of cattle rustling goes on by gentleman's agreement. Where there are no fences, you round up all the cattle you can find. If someone comes along and says, "That one is mine," you simply ask him to prove it. And, of course, where there is no brand, he can't.

But a fellow should not be greedy, also by gentleman's agreement. Steal your cows, but be sure and steal them from the right people—those who are so far away they'll never find out.

That's the way it used to be. Now all this immorality is changing. Not so much because of a change of heart, though, but because we are building corrals and fencing pastures. We're branding our cattle and keeping closer control of them by drilling more water wells, since cattle will seldom stray more than ten miles from known water sources.

Our first mustering at Anna Plains netted 2,673 head of

The new way—Mustering at Anna Plains.

cattle, a few wild horses, and some donkeys. Upward of 20,000 head remained on the station for the simple reason that we could not catch them.

The rainfall at Anna Plains is light, averaging about eight or so inches a year. During The Wet when the native grasses spring up, the cattle gain about half a pound a day. During The Dry, they lose about a quarter of a pound a day. Obviously, the answer to beef production in these parts is water. Since we bought the property, we have sunk a number of new wells, most of which are pumped by windmills. At last count there were eighty of them but even that is not enough. Cattle will travel as far as ten miles to water, but they walk off a lot of meat along the way. Having water within five miles or less of where they graze is better. So we are sinking wells to establish a network of water holes within a few miles of each other. When the system is complete, the cattle will have water and feed within a five-mile parameter—and they had better get fat!

Only two sides of the Anna Plains Station are fenced. There is no fence across the outback side where it vanishes into the desert and there is no fence on the Indian Ocean front. Most of the cattle are wild and when we "muster," which is Australian for roundup, we resort to a number of interesting ruses. Domesticated cows and cows with calves are used as gentling decoys. Eight cowboys, usually aborigines, work our muster. They drive a herd of about 150 of the decoying animals to the mustering area and there they camp overnight.

A cowboy in Australia is called a ringer. On a muster, each ringer takes a string of four horses. He has to have remounts because of the great distances they travel. His "swag," or workbag, consists of a canvas to sleep on, one or two pillows, extra socks, and trousers. A truck carrying food and other supplies follows the ringers. The usual menu is beef and vegetables boiled in a five-gallon can. On a good day, the cook may concoct a curry with rice for variety. They make bread called damper out of flour, baking powder, salt, and water and cook it in a pan directly over the hot coals.

Ringer to guest: *"Y' don't get damper like that at the Waldorf, mate!"*

To attract the wild cattle and get them moving, the ringers sometimes build grass fires. When the wild cattle start moving, the domesticated animals are herded to surround them and then the ringers start a stampede in the direction of the home station. If wild cattle break out of the herd they are either whip-driven back into it or chased until they are exhausted, then tailed down, tied, and trucked to the holding corral—if you can catch them. To placate the wild cattle, the domesticated cows stay in the corrals with them through the brief holding period before they are shipped to the Broome killing plant. Nevertheless, despite this domesticating influence and despite extra feed and abundant water, the wild bullocks lose as much as 150 pounds during that restless period before they are shipped to a slaughter station. The longer they are kept in captivity the more weight they lose. I guess they pine away from homesickness. Apparently freedom is as important to these animals as it is to man.

One persistent enemy of the wild cattle is the dingo. This clever dog will lope along behind a calf until it is exhausted and then attack. Usually it bites off the calf's ears and tail and if the calf manages to escape with its life it is doomed to exist without any protection from the incessant swarm of bush flies.

I've already mentioned how a crocodile can drag a cow into a pool and drown it. But in Australia another enemy of cattle, oddly enough, is the rat. These vicious rodents move occasionally like a plague through the country destroying everything in their paths. They eat the roots of the grass, and they eat boots and saddles and clothing. They not only destroy the feed, but foul the ground and leave it repulsive to cattle. There is no known successful way to deal with a rat plague. You can kill them by the thousands but still they come. Where they come from and where they go I haven't been able to find out; no one seems to know.

Since the distance from Anna Plains to Broome is too great to allow the animals to be trail-driven without their losing considerable weight, truck trains are used to move them over the corrugated dirt roads to the killing station where the meat

The old way—Start of an overland drive.

is packaged and held in refrigeration before shipment by sea to the markets. Some meat is being shipped seven hundred miles by air to ports as far away as Derby or Wyndham, and from there it is carried by ship to the world markets.

I had a chance to visit the killing station at Broome where outback cattle from the area, including our own, are trucked in for slaughter.

I was fascinated by the grim efficiency of mechanized killing as the beasts of the outback come to their last muster. They are held in a killing pen and moved forward, one by one, with scarcely a pause, down the assembly line of slaughter. The animals are killed, disembowled, skinned, and quartered as they move from specialist to specialist along a system of overhead trolley lines. After quartering, the meat is boned out and the fat removed for the rendering vats. After the meat is cooled, it is packed in corrugated boxes and stored in a freezing plant to await the arrival of the next refrigerated ship.

I noticed the high percentage of cows awaiting slaughter in the killing pen as opposed to the steers one would find in an American slaughterhouse.

When I asked a killing-plant official to explain this ratio his answer was direct and to the point.

"It's a fact, mate. We kill more 'she' stuff than steers because they are easier to catch in the muster. The strong ones get away and the weak ones get caught and brought to us."

I looked around the killing pen and noticed many cows that were pregnant and heavy with calf. I turned to my Australian guide again and asked, "Could you guess at the percentage of pregnant cows out of each one hundred cattle brought in?"

"Oh, I'd say about fifty or so, including a few wild mares, donkeys, and an occasional kangaroo—we kill anything they catch and bring to us," he boasted.

"And the unborn calves in the pregnant cows," I persisted. "What do you do with that meat?"

Somebody was calling for my guide and he gave me his answer while going away. "Hell, mate," he laughed, "there's nothing wrong with unborn calf—damned sight more tender than those old bulls in the next pen."

I was left to ponder the rough and ready techniques of outback cattle-raising where the quick and the nimble steers survive and cows and unborn calves supply the meat for pampered pets around the world. And come to think of it, unborn veal could be superior to some of the overage steak I've had in Los Angeles recently.

On a hot Sunday afternoon while I was at Anna Plains, a group of us was sitting on the veranda at the station headquarters. Chuck Denny, the manager, was telling me about one of the girls on the place who had been bitten by a wild dingo. He had driven her to Broome for treatment and it took him seven hours over the miserable roads to get her to a doctor. He asked me if I could use my influence with the government to get the road to Broome improved. I started to say I would do what I could when he interrupted me with, "Hey! Isn't that a Greyhound bus outside?"

A Greyhound bus! I went to the window and sure enough, there it was.

A girl in one of the front seats got out and when she saw me she said, "My God! It's Art Linkletter!"

And I said, "My God—it *is* a Greyhound bus!"

She couldn't have been any more surprised at seeing me than I was at seeing that familiar American symbol. I had seen some of these buses in Sydney and knew that they ran between cities of the populated southeast, but I couldn't imagine what one was doing away out here at Anna Plains.

The driver explained that his passengers were Australian tourists from the East Coast having a look at the wild West. And then he said, "I'd like to get permission from the manager to buy some water and camp here overnight."

"Sorry," I said, "the manager's not here, but if it's OK with the owner you can stay."

"Who's the owner?" he wanted to know.

"I'm one of them," I replied, "so help yourself to water and make yourselves at home."

The Australian hospitality toward a passing stranger is like California was in the days of the great rancheros. You give him food and a place to refresh himself and sleep and in turn he gives you news of the outside world. I'm amazed at how spontaneous this attitude is when you are in an area as isolated as Anna Plains, even if you've been there only a short time.

Eleven Americans and Australians, including a teacher for the children, and forty-three native aborigines, live and work on the Anna Plains Station. The bush region around the area has been the ancestral home of this particular tribe of aborigines for centuries. Many of the cattle stations of the north would not be able to function if it weren't for the aborigine ringers. They are the only ones who can stand the heat and they are the only ones who will do the rugged, dusty, difficult job of mustering for the wages outback cattlemen can afford to pay. They get from six to nine dollars a week, plus keep, depending on their abilities. We pay the aborigine girls and women who work on the station from one to three dollars a week. Each has her own job to do. For example, one is in charge of the chickens and is called the egg woman; she refers to chicken feed as "chickee tucker." The one who is charged with the vegetable garden, for some reason I don't know, is called the pussycat. Others are individually assigned to kitchen, dining room, and bedroom, and two women divide the work of taking care of the lawn. Every aborigine at age sixty gets a pension check regularly from the government. One of the women on the place, whose name, believe it or not, is Pussy Board Jagot, gets twenty-four dollars a month. I would guess she is around sixty-five or seventy years old—even she isn't sure. An older man we call Frankenstein gets a pension and he also collects pensions for the four old women who live with him. Nobody has ever quite figured out what the relationships are in this situation, but there is no doubt about who handles the money.

The aborigine ringers are marvelous horsemen. Though he never saw a horse until the white man came, the aborigine, like his Indian counterpart in America, took to the horse as if it had been an integral part of his heritage.

The Australian horse is very different from the American quarter horse. He is inclined to be leggy with high, sharp withers, and he is not "broken" to the saddle as the quarter horse is. Instead, he is "gentled," which means he is run around and around a stock compound at the end of a rope. Then he is "sack whipped," a gentle way of getting him used to a saddle, and snubbed so that he never learns to buck.

At Anna Plains we have a herd of about two hundred domestic horses, and quite a few wild horses no one has been able to touch so far. The first horses arrived in Australia more than a hundred years ago aboard a ship commanded by a Captain Brumby—so, logically, wild horses are called brumbies.

Australian saddles are not like our western saddle, either. They are an adaptation of the English saddle, though heavier and more awkward. They have no skirts, no cantle, and no horn. The seat is narrow and padded and has a somewhat mushy feeling when you sit on it. The stirrups are steel and they do not have tapaderos (stirrup guards). Almost all the horses have sores or "burns" that leave scars on their withers where the saddle rides too high and too far forward.

The Australian ringer uses his version of a lariat, but he does not snub it down to a horn like American cowboys do. Instead he ties one end of his rope to a steel ring on the left side of the saddle. It works out well, but I don't think it allows the control that one has with the American saddlehorn.

Another Australian variation is the practice of "tailing" to stop or turn a cow or steer that has broken away from a range herd or mob in the outback. The American cowpuncher would use his lariat to leg- or head-rope the runaway animal. Not the Aussie ringer. His technique does not involve the lariat. It is a sort of reverse bull dogging and he calls it tailing.

Tailing is done at breakneck speed while both the escaping animal and the rider and horse are running flat out. The Aussie rider races up behind the cow until he reaches a flank position on the side. At this point he reaches from the saddle and takes a firm, one-handed grip on the cow's tail. With an uplift heave he throws the animal off balance and brings her crashing to the ground. It is very similar to the method practiced by the rough-riding gauchos on the Argentine plains of South America.

CHAPTER SEVENTEEN

Anna Plains Fancy

We were not far into the Anna Plains project before we realized that the big problem here was going to be water—the lack of it. It was soon clear that our most vital and pressing need was for an irrigation system that would enable us to grow pasture or supplemental dry feed. We couldn't hold the cattle in paddocks even for the few days before shipping without something to feed them. And to grow feed we had to have water. There were some wells operating near the station headquarters, pumped by windmills, but we had no storage facilities. What we sorely needed, and quick, was a tank, an engine-propelled pump, and a pipeline system.

We got busy immediately and ordered materials for the irrigation system from a company in Perth, twelve hundred miles south, with the hope that we could get them to Anna Plains before The Wet washed out the roads. But the fates had long since decided that our adventures in Australia were not to be easy, and the rains came while the trucks were on the road. They were bogged down again and again and it was six long months before we finally got the equipment delivered to the station and the irrigation program started. By this time I was beginning to wish I had never heard of that Horatio Alger guy.

The system we engineered and finally put into operation is

Anna Plains Homestead.

designed to water fifty acres. You can imagine the enormity of the task we have before us when you consider that the station encompasses several hundred thousand farmable acres!

Of the bores which have been sunk along this northwestern coastline, some have water temperatures in excess of ninety degrees. Depending on the depth of the bore, the water flows at temperatures ranging from tepid to near boiling. I tested water gushing from a bore in the center of the town of Broome and it was almost too hot for the human skin to stand. An amazing thing is that despite the depth of the wells and the near-boiling temperature of the water, small fish are frequently found in the outflow. Where these creatures come from is a mystery. They are a species altogether different from other freshwater fish and are adapted to temperatures and minerals that would kill other marine life. They quickly die if put in ordinary freshwater.

There are several depth levels from which usable water can be obtained at Anna Plains. Shallow wells pumped by windmills and capable of supplying cattle troughs can be brought in at about thirty feet. Deep bores with artesian pressure may be reached at levels between fifteen hundred and three thousand feet.

Our first deep bores came in with artesian pressure at something below twelve hundred feet. The latter are expensive but they are essential if the million-acre property is to produce its potential. As it is now, at least 50 percent of the Anna Plains acreage is outside the zone of grazing productivity.

Before we came to Anna Plains, no one had tried to grow grain crops or supplemental cattle feed in this part of Australia. We are "giving it a go" and if we are successful, as I am confident we will be, it will be a tremendous step forward for the country. Without this supplemental feed, only the tough, inbred, shorthorn beef cattle can survive. They forage for their feed the year around from the sparse native grasses and the scrub. Following the short three-month season of The Wet there is plenty of feed, but the other nine months of the year the cattle have to subsist on whatever skimpy dry feed they can find. The death rate, as you might expect, is discouragingly high.

With a successful program for raising supplemental feed, beef production can be improved tremendously. Selected animals can be isolated in compounds and fattened for the market, while cows carrying unborn calves can be strengthened for a better strain of progeny.

In addition to water, getting the right kind of manpower at such a remote place as Anna Plains poses serious problems. There are no close neighbors, businesses, entertainment, or schools. Consequently, even if you pay them well, getting good men to come and work the year around is not easy. While we hire some aborigines—and our head stockman, an aborigine, is a jewel—as a rule they are not advanced enough to farm large tracts of land without supervision.

But with water and manpower there is unlimited potential here. The land is adaptable; with a minimum of clearing much of it can be farmed. It will be developed. Money will be made.

Aborigines reacting to the sprinkler system at Anna Plains: *"They'll never get it off the plurry ground!"*

People will become rich. But the work will be tremendous and the development will take years. The $64-million question is: Should irrigation be used to provide supplemental feed for cattle or for growing grain?

If we decide ultimately to concentrate on growing grain, we are going to have to do something about the unbelievable number of kangaroos. In the daytime you don't see them, but at night they come out in droves. You can imagine the damage a dozen of these creatures would do, eating their way through a ripe field of milo.

Another factor to be considered—and this is a standard problem for farmers the world around—is the weather. Unlike Humpty Doo, here hurricanes are common during the monsoon season and, from what the Australians in the Anna Plains area tell me, they do a whale of a lot of damage. According to the priest at the neighboring mission, in 1963 winds of 150 miles an hour were recorded about a half mile from where we have located our first water system. That same 1963 storm struck our nearest neighbor, Rolfe Foxe, and his Nita Downs sheep station, thirty miles north of Anna Plains. The eye of the hurricane which swept across the Indian Ocean turned back upon itself and gale winds piled uprooted bushes against the Nita Downs fences until the pressure tore them completely out of the ground. Blown away, too, were all of the buildings and windmills on the station. Three thousand head of sheep were killed or drowned. Somehow the Foxe family survived and slowly they are rebuilding the station and their flock.

On the forty-mile beach at Anna Plains there is a stark reminder of the violence of such a hurricane. Scattered for five miles along the beach are the bones of eight hundred cattle. Driven by the ferocious wind, they spilled over the dunes and onto the beach at low tide. The hurricane continued to press them, and they walked seaward, there to be caught when the tide turned and raced across three miles of beach—some thirty-six feet from low to high marks! The sharks had the feast of the ages and bones were washed back onto the beach, where they still lie.

The death losses of cattle from natural causes along this coast run as high as 7 to 10 percent. One reason is the age of the cows. Owners tend to keep them until by-death-do-they-part, mainly because of their low worth and the high cost of transporting them to market. Another reason is the lack of proper breeding control. Cows calve the year around and often at the worst time of the year—during The Dry. The water points, furthermore, are so widely spaced that cows have to walk several miles between feed and water. Some of the older, weaker animals also have difficulty getting any water at all because the large, selfish, hostile steers rule the roost at the water holes.

Dusty Smythe, the animal nutritionist for this part of Australia, said there are few cattle under any type of fence control. The roundup is often a trap operation, in which the weakest cattle are caught, while the quick and nimble get away.

Smythe also indicated that because of the lack of professional feeding, watering, and breeding programs, a cow may calve only once every two years. Some of those in the cattle business in these parts evidently don't understand the breeding cycle. They sell what they think is a barren cow when in fact she is with calf. Smythe said that 60 percent of the cows slaughtered at the killing works in Broome were with calf; a shocking statistic for any knowledgeable cattleman.

It all adds up to the need for better management of livestock—more fences, water points, breeding control, and a supplemental source of feed. And these are precisely what we are going to supply.

Our Anna Plains Station is a classic example of the need for cattle control. In all of the near-million acres stretching eastward into the infinity of the desert there is but one enclosed cattle pasture. This is a little holding plot of 100,000 acres where the cattle caught in a general roundup can be held, if you can catch them. Later they can be pushed onto the station headquarters where there are stout holding corrals and loading chutes for the trucks of the cattle trains. As it is now, the only real control centers around the well points where cattle must come in from the outer perimeter grazing areas to get water.

We in the United States are awed by some of the great cattle ranches in Texas and California. The King Ranch, largest in our country, comprises about two million acres. There are any number of ranches that size in Australia, and there are several that are much larger. Coolibah, a cattle station in the Top End, has 4.5 million acres. Also in the Northern Territory is the largest cattle ranch in the world, Alexandria Station, which has 7.25 million acres and stretches 250 miles from north to south, an area as large as Belgium. This tremendous spread runs seventy thousand head of shorthorn cattle. Next to it in size is Victoria River Station, which once was bigger than Holland. Portions of it were sold off and today it is a little less than four million acres. These great ranches have their own aerodromes and their headquarters are towns of considerable size.

At an outback cattle station life is hard and lonely, especially for women and for the "pumpers," who are men employed to live at and supervise the operation of the mill-operated water tanks. Windmills are used at lesser watering points, but not at places where thousands of cattle may water every day. Windmills don't pump sufficient water and a week may go by without sufficient wind to turn the blades. So pumpers live in the vicinity of the tanks and tend the engines which keep them full.

As a rule, pumpers are the outcasts of society—alcoholics, born-losers, ticket-of-leave men, and men who have been driven into these lonely places by booze, women, and the police.

Alan Marshall, in *Walkabout,* tells of an English pumper newly arrived in Australia. "After the derelict had been on the companionless job for a couple of weeks, I saw him at the bore," Marshall recalls. "He looked depressed, and commented as he looked at an unbroken skyline of grass, 'I've got nothing here except a dog and a mouth-organ, and I can't play the mouth-organ because the dog doesn't like it.' "

His captive, lonely life is comparable to that of a lighthouse keeper or to the keeper of an airway beacon in the Utah desert. For companionship he has his dog and the 'roos. For entertainment he has his own voice and those of the raucous cockatoo flocks which each day descend in black and white clouds upon the cattle troughs, there to drink and quarrel. The bottle is his consolation and his hope hangs on the safe arrival of a new supply of whiskey from the home station. He has no plans to go anywhere and little to do save go over his memories.

CHAPTER EIGHTEEN

Pumpers and Aborigines

Until the white man came to Australia, aborigine culture remained primitive, and the aborigine's knowledge was that of the stone-age man. Because they were nomads, they cultivated no crops, preferring to hunt for food with the boomerang and the spear. Among their principal deities was an Earth Mother. One of the religious rituals, called *kunapipi,* included public mating, but was later "purified" by Christian missionaries. Douglas Lockwood, in his book, *I, The Aboriginal,* quotes a member of the Alawa tribe on this subject:

> Kunapipi is devotedly pagan yet deeply religious, and the bane of all Christian missionaries. They have attempted to eradicate it, with about as much success as the early Romans had against Christianity itself. But the ceremonies thought to be most objectionable have been modified and even submissively abandoned to twentieth-century standards of decency.
>
> Soon after the arrival of the first horrified missionaries, the Alawa were induced to drop the ceremony which symbolized fecundity and the relationship of intercourse to the reproduction of the species.
>
> My father's father and his contemporaries became involved in arguments with men of God who were affronted

by their fervid paganism and appalled by some of its manifestations.

"It is wrong that men and women should commit adultery," they were told. "This is one of the commandments of God. To do so in public, as part of a ceremony, is scandalous."

These were strong words. What right did white men have to tell us that we should forsake a ritual which had been practiced by the tribes for more than ten thousand years? What right had they to force upon us a belief in their own God-in-the-sky, the one who frowned upon us most at the moment of our infinite spiritual consummation?

Nevertheless, they won their point. The mission had become our refuge from cruelty and want, and my people were grateful. When my father was a young man, just through his circumcision, the elders told the missionaries: "Kunapipi has been purged. Henceforth it will be inoffensive, a censored ritual which will not break your commandments."

I have often wondered if the magnitude of this concession was ever appreciated.

The kunapipi began as a ritual for tribal women. Subsequently it was recognized by the men as of such profound significance that they not only took it over but banished the women, whose invention it was, except when women are needed to lay down their bodies during the final act of ceremonial intercourse.

All aborigine boys at about the age of nine are circumcised. Today the operation is done with a razor blade, but in other times it was done with an edged stone and must have been terribly painful. After this ceremony—and with the aborigines it is a ceremony—the young boy must sleep with a naked woman, but he must not speak to nor touch her. The purpose is to teach the youngster self-control. Under the circumstances, one doubts if he needs it.

Before the white man came to Australia, of course, the aborigine had no matches and even today they can make a fire in two minutes with a round stick of hard wood called a *budalarr*. This is held upright between the palms with one end pressed firmly against a piece of soft wood. The hands are moved rapidly back and forth spinning the budalarr to create friction. When smoke appears, a little dry grass treated with goanna fat is added. If dry grass is not readily available, it can be found in the mud structures of termites, where it is used to strengthen the walls, as man uses steel to reinforce concrete. Now, with matches and the cigarette lighter available, making fire by hand is a dying art.

But the continued use of goanna fat is dramatic evidence that civilization has not entirely changed the aborigine. The goanna is a foot-long lizard whose fat is widely used by the aborigines as a cureall: at the first sign of any ache or pain they rub it on themselves or eat it.

Today the aborigines are wards of the state, much the same as American Indians. Rations are issued to them periodically by station owners selected by the government. Aborigine girls and women get a new dress every three months, two pairs of underpants, and one slip or petticoat. Men and boys get comparable clothing. And even boys and girls get the weekly ration of tobacco. The meat ration provides one pound per person a day, and the daily sugar ration is one quarter pound per person. The manager of a station may also be empowered by the government to dole out the pensions if there is no more convenient place for him to come. Such moneys are paid a few dollars at a time to prevent the spending of the whole monthly sum at once in the station trading post.

The aborigines at Anna Plains are of desert origin, and the males have a ceremonial custom of wearing 'roo bones in their noses. Inserting it the first time, a very painful operation, is done at puberty as a sign of manhood. They thrust it horizontally through the cartilage that divides the nostrils, and it glistens white like a waxed moustache.

The aborigines on our Anna Plains ranch have their own community kitchen and, in fact, otherwise live their lives pretty much in the ancient communal way. Like most primitive peoples, the women do the heavy and menial work, while the men do the fun things, such as hunting and fishing. It was ever thus until civilization, alas, came along.

The aborigines eat worms and snakes and practically anything that runs or crawls or flies or swims, and whatever food they get they share with one another. They are particularly fond of roasted 'roo. They will kill a buck kangaroo, make a fire, and drag the "old man" back and forth through the hot coals to singe off the hair. Then when the skin is nice and bare, they will bury him in the ground, pile the embers and a layer of dirt over him, and let him cook, like the Polynesians prepare a pig. After three hours the dirt and ashes are pulled away and the entire marsupial is consumed: eyes, ears, intestines—the works.

Another favorite dish of the aborigines is made of fried brains, liver, sweetbreads, "tummick and hunnions" (stomach and onions). Their fondness for animal "innards" was demonstrated to me one day when a large barrimundi fish was caught and the fisherman threw away the stomach. When the aborigines came to buy the coarse fish, they complained because the stomach was missing. They searched the bushes for it, hoping to add it as flavoring to their stew, but something or somebody had beaten them to it.

Topping the list of aborigine favorite foods is wild honey. An enterprising aborigine boy will capture a bee in a blossom, attach a bit of colored feather to the bee's body, and follow it back to the hive. Australia's desert honeys have a rich, exotic flavor—a blend of desert blooms similar to our own mesquite, wild sage, and buckwheat. When flowers are out of season the hundreds of eucalyptus and acacia provide abundant nectar for the nomadic bees.

Other insects collect and store nectar in the living bodies of ants, which serve as underground storage tanks. These ants, whose only job is to store the honey, swell to the size of a small marble and spend their lives pretty much as cows. Worker ants remove the honey from a nipple and feed it to the young. But the aborigines know of this procedure and they dig up the swollen ants and pop them into their mouths as we do brandy-filled chocolate-covered cherries.

These people are not materialists in any sense of the word.

Possessions mean little to them. And they are unable to understand the white man's desire to possess land and put a fence around it, or to acquire and own anything beyond his daily requirements. The aborigine's communal philosophy was well expressed by Tommy, a stockboy at the station. Anna Plains had been the traditional home of Tommy's tribe since the beginning of dream time and I asked him if he considered that his people really belonged to the land. The boy's answer came in the pidgin English widely spoken in the area: "I not know," he said. "My people not think like white people—all time white people want to belong things. We not belong land. Land belong us. My people belong along all things here—we belong along land and water and tucker. We belong along together—all things."

For more than a century the explorers, settlers, traders, and missionaries who came to Australia and the Pacific islands were confronted with the nearly hopeless task of conversing with the natives. There were more than three hundred tribes on the continent, no two of which spoke the same language. Furthermore, not one of their languages was recorded. It was out of necessity therefore that pidgin English developed to become a common means of communication.

Julius Kruttschnitt, of the Mount Isa Mines, gave me a yellowed dictionary of pidgin that was used in conversations with the natives of northern Australia at the turn of the century. Its foreword includes a long list of *don't*s to guide the white man in his dealings with the natives. (It should be noted that then, as now, all male aborigines are referred to as "boys," while females are identified as "lubras" or "gins.")

Some of the rules cautioned settlers:

1. Don't strike a boy. It is an offense under the native labor ordinance, and this form of attack often leads to rapid retaliation on the boy's part.
2. Don't cast reflections on a boy's parentage. They worship their ancestors.
3. Don't, if you are a woman, allow a houseboy to remove your shoes or wash your underclothing.

4. Don't forget that a native can tell an untruth with just as much candor as a white man.

5. Don't think that if you flirt with a native woman it will be forgotten. It will be a village topic for months and maybe even years to come.

6. Don't lose sight of the fact that a houseboy's weaknesses are sugar, butter, and meat drippings. Watch your stores.

7. Don't, in the presence of idle natives, do any task that a native should do.

8. Don't fail, in giving clothes to a native, to pass along a certificate to this effect, in case he is questioned by police.

9. Don't lose sight of the fact that all natives are human beings and as such have all the sex instincts of an adult white.

Getting back to aborigine-talk, I remember a conversation I overheard between our white Australian cook at Anna Plains Station and a new "boy" just in from the outback desert. When I came into the kitchen the boy was standing in the back door clad in a pair of faded shorts; tribal marks scarred his brown chest. The cook wanted him to go to the station store, some distance away, and fetch certain items. She handed him a list. "You boy," she said, "bringim this pass along store belong tucker."

The boy's brows furrowed. "Missus, me no savvy store belong tucker. Him he stop where?" Translation: "I don't know where the food (tucker) store is. Where is it?"

Gesticulating, the perspiring cook elaborated: "Him store we callim name belong him. He stop close to petrol house."

The boy's eyes lighted with understanding. He nodded happily. "Missus, me savvy where stop him tucker house," he said and padded off to do the errand.

In Broome the owner of a pearling fleet listed some of the pidgin nautical phrases he used to direct a crew of Malaysians and aborigines manning his sailing luggers. The command to anchor a ship is: "Throw away the anchor." "You fassim 'atches" means to cover the hatches. The command to start the hoisting engine is: "Get him upin machine." And to stop,

"Make him machine he die." Asking the helmsman to identify another ship: "Ship him belong whosat?" Reminding the wheelsman to check his course: "Boy belong steer, come looking course." The order to unload the cargo translates easily: "Opium hatches, rausim cargo."

The days of the week are Wonedi, Toodi, Thredi, Fourdi, Fridi, Saturdi, Sundi. Sunday is also called limlumbuy, which means a holiday or a day of rest. A month quite logically is a "moon." A year is "one Christmas." The numerals are one, two, tri, for, fiv, sikex, seven, eight, nine, one-fella-ten. Twenty, by pidgin logic, is two-fella-ten but eleven is one-ten-one while twelve is one-ten-two and so on to nineteen which is one-ten-nine or close-up-to-fella-ten.

The missionaries have long since translated the Bible into pidgin. "Olpella Testament" translates to "Old Fellow Testament," which makes the New Testament, of course, "Newpella Testament."

Julius Kruttschnitt told me of an incident that occurred when a traveling bishop visited one of the Northern Territory missions. The head of the mission was very proud of his houseboy cook and his ability to bake elaborate cakes. He ordered such a cake to honor the visiting prelate. Houseboy Tommy wanted further identification. "What fella him come along name Bishop?" he asked.

"Him fella high up church," the missionary explained. "Him number one boy church. You savvy?"

The cook savvied very well. After a delicious dinner, Tommy came into the dining room bearing a huge, fancily decorated cake. The visiting bishop, you may be sure, was delighted as he read the confectionery inscription: "Hooray! Number One Fella God."

An incredible anachronism is the sight of one of these stone-age people loping into the station out of a trackless desert, clad only in a semi-loin cloth, while forty thousand feet above a modern jetliner speeds along at five hundred miles an hour, with a sophisticated cargo of world travelers drinking champagne and eating filet mignon.

Once I heard an aborigine man take notice of a huge airliner overhead: "Him quick auto car on high road belong sky."

While pidgin English has persisted throughout Australia, Asia, and the South Pacific for more than a hundred years, this musical forerunner of Esperanto is rapidly disappearing. Australia's improved educational program for the aborigines has pretty well reduced pidgin to the outback of the Northern Territory and to outlying islands such as New Guinea. As more and more aborigines are confined to government reservations or absorbed into the white society, it is probable that pidgin English will have disappeared in another quarter of a century.

As pidgin has been diminished by the onslaught of civilization, so too have other colorful means of effective but primitive aborigine communications. The smoke signal codes which used to send messages across the outback to back-of-beyond have all but disappeared. As recently as fifty years ago smoke signals were widely used. The aborigines were able to communicate over great distances in a matter of hours. Detailed information about the nature, the attitude, and the purpose of white exploring parties was known to aborigine tribes weeks ahead of the whites' arrival at any given point. In those days, too, there were many instances when white explorers relied upon the aborigine guides to relay smoke-signaled information about their progress to civilized points on the coast hundreds of miles away. Many times lost explorers and prospectors were located by wandering aborigines who relayed the condition and whereabouts of the lost party to rescuers on the outside using smoke signals.

An aborigine knows only one thing better than perhaps anyone else in the world: how to survive where even animals and insects die.

There is a belief among outback folks that you could blindfold one of these gypsy desert dwellers and fly him to the most inaccessible wilderness and put him down, and he would not only find food and water enough to live, but would unerringly walk out to the nearest settlement as if he were following some invisible map.

"Walkabouts" are an ancient part of dream time aboriginal religion. Each year even the most civilized aborigine gets restless and moody. Finally, he will just vanish for a few weeks or a month. He has gone to shed the restraining, softening habits of civilization, along with his shoes, pants, and shirt, to just "walk about" in the bush, proving to himself and his fellows that he can still live in the old ways.

Most aborigines go barefoot and are seemingly immune to thorns, stones, beestings, and the bites of swarming insects called bities. They keep their bodies quite clean, bathing often when they can, and seem to harbor no fleas or other parasites. Each family tribal unit has its own medicine man or voodoo-priest who tries to cure illnesses by driving away the evil spirits. They sleep with their dogs, for whom they have great affection. Also, the dogs keep the aborigines warm when the weather is chilly, and the temperature of a cold night is described in terms of a one-dog, two-dog, or three-dog night.

When we were taking the aborigine census on the ranch at Anna Plains, I asked an old man what his name was. "Demon," he said, "no other."

"How old are you?"

"I proper man when Wyndham bombed," he replied. I took a wild guess and put him down as sixty, as it related to Japanese bombings in World War II.

None of the natives on our place could be definite about his age, so we set down an appropriate age for each. All were very pleased to be given an age and each was delighted with the age that was chosen for him. We considered assigning each of them a birthday, so he or she could celebrate it, but thought such a civilized custom might cause more confusion and cupidity than joy.

When I asked a woman the name of her deceased husband, she did not reply, and I learned later that it is taboo to mention the name of the dead.

They are very strict about their superstitions. Women must never, under pain of a mysterious, inward-born death, see certain religious rites.

I was taken to see a "corroboree" ceremony by a high government official in the Northern Territory one year, but my wife, Lois, had to sit in a hot, fly-filled truck while I hiked a mile into the bush to watch the dance. The men were painted white in weird designs and shook spears at other grotesquely daubed natives sneaking through the brush toward the sacred spot marked by a circle of whitewashed stones. They chanted unintelligible songs and seemed oblivious of my presence. I asked my guide what would have happened had we brought Lois. He seemed surprised at the suggestion and said, "Oh, but she might die!" I scoffed at this, and he admitted that perhaps he'd been carried away by things he had seen.

He told me of a native girl who, by chance, had seen the taboo religious sticks while on a special visit to a museum in Sydney. She had promptly fallen into a trance and no modern medical aids could help her. She was slowly dying in spite of all white man's medicine, until a bright aide suggested telling her that the museum pieces were really fakes. She immediately got better and ran off and disappeared.

When white men first came to Australia, they found the aborigines to be people of the most primitive stone-age culture. They had no permanent houses or settlements, no pottery, and no domestic animals save the half-domesticated dingoes that hunted for the women. The aborigines probably brought the dingoes with them when they came to Australia from the north over long-since-submerged land bridges. Aborigines consider dingoes to be semisacred, perhaps the incarnation of spirits, and they are fiercely protective of them. An aborigine will not kill a dingo puppy nor tell a white man where a wild dingo den is located. If a dingo becomes vicious in an aborigine camp, he will be "tried" by a council and if found guilty, staked out on a beach at low tide and left there to be drowned by the incoming water. In this way, the aborigine is absolved of personal guilt in the dingo's death. An aborigine will say the dog was well the last time he saw him; it must have been the tide that killed him.

Thus the dingo occupies a secure place in the social structure of the aborigines. They are addressed by their owners, generally women, as if they were members of the family. And if the dingo misbehaves—for instance, bites—he is treated in kind: the offended person does not beat the dog; he bites him. Aborigine punishment is based, quite literally, on the philosophy of "an eye for an eye."

Dingoes dig mice from burrows and have been known to catch birds on the wing. Nocturnal animals in the wild state, they spend the hot days sleeping in shadow and venture forth at night to forage. If captured as puppies, they make good pets —at least for a while, until the call of the wild causes them to run away.

Government trappers are employed to hunt the dingo and keep him from proliferating, but after a century of poisoning, shooting, and trapping, man has failed to conquer this adaptive animal. Despite the fact that there is a high price on his head in those parts of Australia where he takes a heavy toll of flocks and herds, the dingo still abounds as indestructible as our coyote.

CHAPTER NINETEEN

The New Eldorado

Australia is now something more than the mysterious "land down under" where stone-age aborigines wandered across limitless deserts, cuddly koala bears munched eucalyptus leaves sleepily, and a handful of remittance men, outcasts, and adventurers clustered along its southeastern coastline grubbing out a meager living. Today Australia is a nation undergoing a remarkable transformation. It has become a land of bright opportunity where modern cities, space-age industry, vast mineral resources, and, above all, promise are attracting the attention of the world.

There is no question but Australia is the new Eldorado. That great continent, which for centuries has hoarded her riches, is now disgorging them. Australia's time has come.

My friend, Edgar Kaiser, whose company, Kaiser Industries, has invested nearly $300 million* in Australia, said the other day that the continent's natural resources are possibly the greatest in the world. And from Europe, the United States, and elsewhere men with know-how and companies with resources are bringing the knowledge and money necessary to develop these resources.

You might ask why Australia has not been exploited before. Well, for one thing, in terms of civilization she is a very young

* U.S. currency.

country. For another, there are comparatively few people there. Man has not swarmed over this land as he has other parts of the world. Communities in the interior are few and far between and distances are forbidding.

Some of the vast mineral deposits which have been "discovered" recently have been known by the Australians to exist for years: chromite, for example, was reported in the State of Victoria in 1868, and the red iron-containing rock of Western Australia was seen from the air years ago; but until now, for lack of money and accessibility, neither claim had been proven. Without accessibility, without technology, and without markets many of the known resources were considered to have no value.

But now, with money and the technological and population explosions, there is a terrific demand for gold, silver and lead and zinc and chromite and phosphate and uranium and manganese and bauxite and nickel and iron, all of which, it has been discovered, are abundant in the land down under.

In Anna Plains, Esperance, and other stations in the middle and far north of Western Australia, I have invested with my good friends Allen Chase, Jack Wrather, Albert E. and Jack Schwabacher, Earl Slick of Texas, and John Brown Cook of Connecticut. The station at Fitzroy is a 765,000-acre spread with a big river running through it, and we have several thousand head of cattle there. Another, Dunham, is a million-acre station near the famed Ord River cotton-growing area where we run another eight to nine thousand head, along with the wild camels I described earlier. These ranches are in the truly isolated outback and will be a number of years in developing; but each year the demand for meat grows, and we can produce it there more economically than any other place on earth.

Ranchers who have gone into the northern territories are flabbergasted to find that properties of one, two, and even four million acres are available for very little money. The King Ranch of Texas pays to the Government of Australia a yearly rental fee of $1.12 per square mile for a 4,700-square-mile property there. It costs about $25 a head to raise and market cattle, which is almost one-third the cost in the United States. And most important to many, there is plenty of space and a sympathetic tax structure. Capital expenditures of up to 120 percent of the cost can be written off in five years. There is a seven-year loss-carry-forward available.

I believe Australia represents the greatest opportunity for agricultural investment anywhere in the world. It is no secret that the world's population growth is accelerating and that the need for food is increasing proportionately. Food in many areas of the world has always been in short supply, and it now seems that within the next thirty-five years mankind is going to need twice as much food as he needs today. Northern and Western Australia offer thousands of square miles of virgin land that can produce much of that food. All that the land needs to be made productive is money, management, water, and fertilizer.

The recent completion of a pilot dam to harness the waters of the Ord River near Kunanurra in Western Australia has resulted in opening a fabulous agricultural empire. Now during The Dry the land can be irrigated. In an area which used to be alternately flooded in one season and burned out the next, two and three thousand pounds of cotton are being raised to the acre—truly astounding production. And don't think Arizona and California cotton farmers haven't found out about it: they're migrating there in numbers. I walked through stands of sugarcane that produce seventy to eighty tons of sugar an acre, which is better than they do in Hawaii. With water control, rice farmers are also prospering in this area, and I must say that, recalling our experience at Humpty Doo, I look upon their beautiful paddies with admiration and a smidgen of envy.

Two other great Kimberley rivers, the Fitzroy and the Margaret, during the monsoon season carry more than one million cubic feet of flood runoff water a second. Once these wild giants are tamed with dams and reservoirs, other vast areas of the north will be open to the production of cotton and an infinite variety of tropical and semitropical fruits and vegetables.

Another exciting possibility lies in the untapped resource of power exerted by the phenomenal tides which rise and fall along the coasts and up the rivers of northern Australia. There the rise and fall of the tides is as much as thirty-six feet, and experts have estimated that if these tides could be harnessed, they would generate enormous amounts of electricity.

The largest government undertaking is the Snowy Mountains Scheme in New South Wales. It was begun in 1949 and won't be completed until 1974. It will cost almost one billion dollars. The project involves three thousand square miles of mountainous country. There are to be eight dams, one hundred miles of tunnels, and more than eighty miles of aqueducts, plus ten hydroelectric plants, some of them hundreds of feet underground. When completed, the complex will produce three million kilowatts of peak load power and irrigate one thousand square miles. The American Society of Civil Engineers calls the Snowy Mountains Scheme "one of the five wonders of the world."

Yes, the whole of Australia is changing. Whereas much of it used to be a desolate land of flooding Wet and searing Dry, it now has uranium, nickel, coal, manganese, and bauxite mines; and by controlling the water of the rivers and opening up sources of stored underground water, it is adding to Australia's importance as world supplier of food, leather, and wool. Even at dry Alice Springs, situated in almost the absolute center of the continent, a thousand miles south of Darwin, and one of the toughest places to farm on earth, ranches are producing improved breeds of cattle.

I asked a lady who lives on a station near Alice Springs why she did not move to Perth or Esperance, where it rains beautifully and where things are green. She wiped the dusty perspiration from her face and said, "Oh, gad no. This is the place for me. I'd never get the feel of easy living."

That attitude is typical of Australians. The tougher it is, it seems, the better they like it. These people are indomitable; they are strong and kind and moral and iconoclastic. Come to think of it, they are not unlike us Americans. Perhaps that explains the feeling of mutual admiration which exists between us.

Referring to droughts which plague Australia from time to time (one during their summer period, 1965–66, when fifteen million sheep and one million cattle were lost, cost the country more than a billion dollars), W. A. Beattie, an Aussie friend who lives in Melbourne, told me that some of the Australian's innate caution is due to these dry periods.

"These drys create a philosophy that prosperity is something temporary," Bill said. "Every family that buys a home pays any mortgage off quickly. In this way the family is assured of security. An Aussie does not accept credit readily on that account and prefers unencumbered ownership—just in case! This seems to me to be a basic difference between us Aussies and you Yanks. But we are tending to change. As we get more diversification into the community and spread our risks by industrial development we are beginning to take more risks."

I stress the wonderful opportunities of Western Australia and the Northern Territory, but I do not mean to neglect the other four states of the country: New South Wales and Victoria in the south, by far the most populated areas; Queensland in the northeast; and South Australia. In all states there are equally favorable opportunities, although Western Australia may offer more chances on the wheel of fortune than any of the others. It is the largest of the political divisions and, with only about 800,000 residents, is so underpopulated it seems like an unexplored world. Migrants it needs, even more than the other states. It needs eyes to find its treasures and hands to get them out.

But the key word, as Harold Holt told us at Allen Chase's house in Bel Air those many years ago, is money. Great gobs of capital are needed to exploit what this huge country has to offer—to buy the machines and pay the wages and bridge the distances. Everything in Australia is not king-size, but giant-size, including the way one has to think. More than fifteen billion tons—that's right, fifteen billion tons—of high-grade iron ore have been discovered in Western Australia and there are lower grade ores in the neighborhood by the cubic mile. Japan alone has committed itself to purchase four billion dollars' worth of this material over the next twenty-five years. And just think—all of this wealth is owned by less than twelve million Aussies, hardly more people than reside in metropolitan New York.

So Australia is the land of opportunity. But what about it for the average American?

I get scores of letters every week asking this question from people who want to pull up stakes and go to Australia to stay. The writers range from a retired sea captain to a college boy. Their money requirements vary from a "bare living for the rest of my life" to "a chance to get rich if I work hard." Officials of the Mormon Church in Salt Lake City recently asked my advice about sending some of their fine young people down under to take up land. Many of the correspondents wonder if life in Australia would be more wholesome for their kids. Others want to escape the violence of the city streets in our dangerously overcrowded cities. And still others think Australia would be a good place to be in the event of an atomic war.

Answering these people is one of my more serious problems. What can I say to a cotton farmer in Texas who is fed up with federal regulations, government cutbacks, or miserable competitive marketing conditions? How can I honestly reply to a retired schoolteacher who has "twenty thousand dollars* to invest in something in Australia"?

Everything depends upon the personality, adaptability, and background of each person. Many—perhaps I should say most—Americans have been spoiled by a style of life never experienced by any other people in the history of the world. We have been conditioned to get too much too soon too often, and to pay for it later. We have lost the ability to entertain ourselves, read quietly, converse seriously, and stay put.

Generally, I warn that Australia is basically a pioneering country. Americans should not go there expecting to pick oranges off the trees or gold from the ground. Even in major cities, houses often lack modern plumbing, central heating,

* U.S. currency.

and most assuredly air conditioning. The after-hours services that Americans take for granted—nighttime shopping hours, for example—do not yet exist there to any sizable degree. Factory work pays only sixty or sixty-five dollars a week, which is far less than American workers are accustomed to. The pace of life is slow, which proves frustrating to people from the United States. It takes time to get a lease or title to land, and it might take more than two years to get your own telephone.

Significantly, Australian immigration agents are in every large city in Europe, but not one is stationed in the United States. For the last decade, United States dollars have been flowing to Australia (the rising investment tide has now surpassed $1.2 billion), but until very recently, Americans themselves have been notably reticent about going down under to invest their skills and energies. Last year, about 6,600 people from the United States went there to settle or look over the prospects. So far in 1968, this number has been surpassed. Since the end of World War II, about 44,000 Americans have migrated, and most of them have gone to stay.

Distance—7,000 miles from Los Angeles to Sydney—and the high cost of getting there have been major obstacles to American migration. Now Australia will advance $160 (it costs $560* to fly one way) to any American who will agree to remain at least two years, or refund the money if he doesn't. Where to live and what to do when they get there is, of course, another major deterrent to making the move.

Here again, the answer is dependent upon many, many factors. Wages are from one-half to one-third what they are in the United States. There is uniformity of salaries throughout Australia; wages are regulated by state law, and they vary little from one state to the next. Australia has 99.2 percent employment, with the few who are not employed classed as unemployable. Naturally, competition to get workers is keen. Skilled workers are at a real premium; the more skilled the greater the need. And yet, truck drivers cannot expect to earn much more than $45 a week; toolmakers, $60; plumbers about the same;

* U.S. currency.

and farm workers, $40. An insurance man whose starting salary in California would be $6,000* would do well to start at $2,500* a year in Australia.

And surprisingly, costs are sometimes comparable to or higher than those in Los Angeles. That is, if you want to live in the same manner to which you have become accustomed. Everything technical or mechanical, like television sets, automobiles, and appliances are much costlier because manufacturing and distribution costs are much higher in a country of only 11.6 million inhabitants. A recent survey found that the cost of living in Sydney is 20 percent higher than in San Francisco.

Income taxes are generally higher, and there are many taxes new to Americans: 25 percent on cars; $12 a year for each television set you own; and $5.50 for each radio. Down payments on homes are higher. Interest rates are higher. Since there are no savings-and-loan companies, one cannot easily borrow money for home buying. But there are no capital gain taxes, and there are no state income taxes.

Many Americans who go to Australia have trouble adjusting to the fact that the pace in Australia is comparatively slow. A few disenchanted American families turn around and go home on that account after only a short stay in Australia. They dislike the way of life that appeals to so many Australian men: beer, gambling, going to horse races, and working at just one pace—slow. Australians, on the other hand, reply that it is the way they want to live.

One thing Americans must accept is that Australia, for the average person, is not a land where you can get rich in a hurry. But the prospects of success are excellent if the newcomer is willing to work hard and be patient.

After ten years my own property in Esperance carries forty thousand head of Merino sheep, five hundred head of Angus cattle, five hundred head of Hereford cattle, and we are farming about one thousand acres of wheat, barley, and soybean. On the invested capital, we net about 15.6 percent per year which is a handsome profit in farming. The land has appreci-

* U.S. currency.

ated in these ten years from fifty cents an acre for raw land to about fifteen dollars per acre. Paved roads, telephones, schools, a small shopping district, and neighbors like David Rockefeller have all come to our district.

Having a part in this pioneer development has to be one of the greatest thrills of my not uneventful life. Betting my money, spending my time on jets, and worrying about crops, wild dogs, water, disease, world wool markets, and the like have all been a new way of life for me. Overseeing a million-dollar property from half a world away seems like an "Arthur in Wonderland" fantasy, but it has worked remarkably well.

Most of us in show business are proud of our scrapbooks filled with clippings about ourselves. But one of my treasured newspaper souvenirs is the one from the South Australian *Stock Journal,* dated February 22, 1967. The headline reads: "Linkletter's Place Is the Showplace of West Australia." The story goes on to say: "Increased stocking rates, a basic rotational grazing system, with maximum use of perennial grasses, and culling and breeding selection by computer, combine to make 'Linkletter's Place' the show property of the West." I don't expect many city folks to dig this country talk, and it may not seem very glamourous to my Hollywood colleagues, but this is heady stuff coming from the authoritative and conservative *Stock Journal,* and I must add in the light of a decade of outback pioneering, a lot more meaningful to me than a story in *Variety* about Linkletter's personally wowing them in Toronto or New York.

Australians make no secret of their dislike for people who push, work too hard, go too fast, and are too obviously interested in success and status. Most Australians are a little less spontaneous and outgoing than most Americans. This may be because they still have a little more British reserve and understatement in their makeup, and it may also be that the harsh beginnings of their country have bred into them a certain disbelieving quality which tends to make them take things with a grain of salt. For this reason, if for no other, the Australian tends to be resistant to propaganda and the "hard sell." Perhaps also partly because of their early history, Australians tend to be a little rough and abrupt in manner, which when combined with their somewhat sardonic attitude to authority and position—especially to pretentiousness—may be a little disconcerting at first.

Since my own particular pet peeve is hypocrisy in any form, this may be why I am so fond of Australians and their plain, hard-nosed view of things.

But the quality which most of all I find admirable in the Australian is his dependability. Of course, everyone there doesn't possess it, and some of our early station help was testimony to that, but I believe you will find it at least as often as you will in any other country in the world.

To many, Australia is still a land where everything seems upside down. Our summer is their winter; their tropical climate is to the north while ours is to our south; their language often sounds stranger than a truly foreign tongue; and whatever the time in the United States, it is always tomorrow in Australia.

What kind of people do they want in Australia? Well, for a beginning, they prefer them young. Australia itself is a young nation and 40 percent of the population is under twenty-one. They prefer immigrants to be Caucasian or Latin. Persons of European stock are welcomed, while Afro-Asians are not. Though this white Australian policy is supported by most of the population and by two of the country's three political parties, no Australian is proud of it. In fact, it is a private subject they do not like to discuss with outsiders. Their ancestors and they have come here and hacked out a home for themselves and they don't want willingly to create any problems. Unlike others of European origin who have adapted themselves in a torrid climate, the Australians have done most of their own manual labor; they have resisted the temptation to bring in cheap Oriental labor by the shipload, as Africans were brought to America.

The total non-European population of Australia is less than one percent; thus they have no racial friction like we have here in the United States. Because there is as yet no racial problem, racial relations with visitors of various hues are harmonious. Africans and Orientals in no way threaten the Aussie's way of life, so they are made to feel at home when they come as visitors. Nevertheless, Australia's white-only policy is an obstacle to her influence in the Pacific and to her expanding trade with Asian countries. It is changing slowly but surely.

As a consequence of immigration during this century, one-sixth of Australia's population is foreign-born. The influx accelerated after World War II when a program to bring in 100,000 immigrants a year was adopted. Under this program some 50 percent have come from the United Kingdom, 19 percent from southern Europe, 10 percent from the Slav countries, and 14 percent from northern Europe.

Australians like the last group the most—Germans, Scandinavians, and Dutch. Those immigrants from southern Europe —that is, the Latins and the Greeks and the Yugoslavs—are considered less desirable. One reason for this is that these people tend to concentrate in urban areas rather than migrate to rural frontiers. The language barrier has a great deal to do with this attitude, and religion plays a part also.

Australia is predominantly a Protestant country, while many of those who come from southern Europe are Roman Catholic. Another factor is that those from southern Europe to a great extent come not to stay but to fill their pockets and return home. It is slightly ironical, I think, that the Australian attitude toward those immigrants who come from the British Isles is inclined to be critical. They particularly dislike Britons, or anyone else, who bring with them an air of prosperity or superiority.

If you are healthy and go to Australia, you won't have much trouble getting a job. There is demand for workers in practically every field. The unemployment rate is the lowest of any major nation. Sydney alone has ten thousand more jobs than people to fill them. And the country can maintain its economic momentum only by taking in new settlers. Despite the 100,000 a year immigration program, which last year fell short of the goal, booming Western Australia, much of which is so like California, has seen immigration drop from 2.5 percent of the population during the fifties to 1 percent in 1966. There is talk—indeed, the Premier of the state himself has suggested—that it may become necessary to allow foreign companies, which are helping in such a big way to develop the territory, to bring in their own workmen, and he does not rule out Asians, since they are the nearest available. Presumably they would come and leave when the job was done, because Australia does not offer freedom of immigration to Asians, not even when they are fellow members of the British Commonwealth.

Paradoxically, more than twelve thousand Asians, principally students, are presently living in Australia to learn many things the Australians can teach them. But there are not anywhere near that many Australian students—in fact there are very few—living in Asia to learn things that Asians could teach them.

As I have said elsewhere in this book, Australia is no place to poor-boy. You will end up working as a laborer and that is no easy way to prosper. Of course, there is always a chance to work your way up the ladder, as John Hagon did, under any circumstances; if you save your money you may make a go of it. But if you are going to get in on the burgeoning prosperity in Australia, you need some wherewithal, some money. And particularly is this true if you want to go into agriculture. If you take money to Australia, where it is so desperately needed, you will share not only in the excitement of development but in the profits as well.

I can't tell you what is going to happen in the next thirty years or so down under, but it will be tremendously important, not only to Australia but to the world. Going there to pioneer is one of the most exciting things a man can do. There you will find great opportunities, a stable government, and a people who are particularly sympathetic to Americans.

Australia is rapidly becoming industrialized. As recently as 1948, every automobile was imported. Today, every other car is Australia-made or assembled. Australia's factories are also turning out locomotives, aircraft, ships, television sets, cosmetics, pharmaceuticals, scientific instruments, and hundreds of other items which compete in the world's markets. By 1971 Australia's recent oil and gas discoveries will make her completely free of imports.

But along with all of the work, there is fun. Australia is a land where holidays are so sacred that they are not necessarily celebrated on the dates they fall, but on Mondays, to give everyone a long weekend.

The Minister for Industrial Development of the State of Western Australia, Charles Court, finds a strong similarity between Australians and Americans. He says, "We are a free and democratic people. We have a vast continent, undivided as to language, nationality, standards, hopes and aspirations, with a good standard of living and an extraordinarily balanced spread of wealth and income. There is a political and economic stability. We are a predominantly private enterprise community with a high degree of home ownership and an appreciation of human rights and values. Ours is a place where contracts will be honored. We come from pioneering and unpampered stock. Are these not the ingredients on which good sound development can be based with confidence? Where else are these ingredients with vast undeveloped resources available in such measure? The answer is: nowhere."

Three of us mere mortals—my partner Clyde Vandeburg, a black aborigine stockman, and I—sat under the twinkling stars on the lawn of the homestead of the Anna Plains Station one night late in 1966. Save for the sound of night birds and the Indian Ocean breeze stirring in an acacia tree, nothing broke the soft silence. The nearest neighbor homestead, Nita Downs, was thirty miles to the north. Having just flown in from Los Angeles, our smog-accustomed eyes were dazzled by the clear atmosphere which magnified the smallest star to the brilliance of a tiny sun. So bright was the Milky Way that it seemed a splash of diamond dust whipped up from the Indian Ocean and sprayed across the black velvet sky. My companions had invited me into the night to witness a miracle—the passing of an orbiting spacecraft.

As we sat on the baked ground waiting, Tommy pointed to the silhouette of a windmill leaning against the western sky and spoke: "He sky fellow, pass along there quick-quick." The stone-age aborigine glanced at the radium dial of his watch and said, "Ten second, he come." And like the biblical wise men we sat there waiting. In the space of three breaths the miracle occurred. A star as blazing bright as the largest in the heavens suddenly appeared between the blades of the still windmill. Even at that great distance the shining satellite confirmed its speed of eighteen thousand miles an hour. It rose steadily toward the apex of the sky, drifted toward the horizon, and as suddenly and smoothly as it had come, blinked out over the eastern horizon.

For several seconds no one spoke. The sight had filled all of us with awe. Tommy was the first to break the silence. "I go many time walkabout," he said, "but never go away Anna Plains." He paused, then added: "I wonder those fellow fly about all place ever have walkabout any place?"

The question came from a mind which has little understanding of the world in which he lives. Since there is so much space in Australia that is empty and unexplored, why, Tommy was asking, do men want to walk about on the moon when they could walk about Australia?

In *The Australian* my friend George Johnson has written: *The one thing that remains constant is the challenge of this country. It is the most exciting thing about Australia. There is still so much to be done. Here, in a world where so many have come to fear the beginning of the end, Australia has come only to the end of the beginning.*

GLOSSARY

Beano (Also Shivoo)	*A convivial party*
Boundary Rider	*A fence rider*
Bush	*Any rural area*
Dingo (dingoes, pl.)	*Australian wild dog—a companion of aborigines*
Drover	*Cow puncher*
Dry (The)	*The nine-month period of unceasing drought and heat after the monsoon*
Flying Doe	*A female kangaroo*
Gin	*An aborigine woman*
Good on You	*Term of approval sometimes used ironically*
Jackaroo	*A young man who looks after sheep on a station*
Joey	*A young kangaroo*
Jumbuck	*A sheep, particularly one with large fleece*
Kelpie	*Type of sheep dog developed in Australia*
Killing Plant	*A slaughter house*
Outback	*Australian back country*
Ringer	*Cowboy*
Smoko	*Coffee break—period of rest*
Strine	*Colloquial speech*
Swag	*Rolled blanket containing personal effects of a hobo or itinerant*
Top End (The)	*The extreme north—Northern Territory*
Tucker	*Food or a meal*

Walkabout	*The aborigine's periodic test of physical prowess when he abandons civilization and exists with his own primitive weapons in the outback*
Wet (The)	*The three-month monsoon period of unceasing rain*